COHERENT CHRISTIANITY

A More Liberating, Less Traveled Way

RONALD PERRITT

© 2019
Published in the United States by Nurturing Faith Inc., Macon GA,
www.nurturingfaith.net.

Library of Congress Cataloging-in-Publication Data is available.

ISBN: 978-1-63528-060-9

All rights reserved. Printed in the United States of America

CONTENTS

Introduction 1

Seeking a New Approach to Coherent Christianity 7
    The Bible as a Divine Oracle:
    A Hypothesis 9
        Factors in the Hypothesis 9
        Background of the Hypothesis 10
        Strengths of the Hypothesis 13
        Weaknesses of the Hypothesis 14
        A "House of Cards" 26

    The Bible as a Collection of Human Documents:
    A Hypothesis 28
        Factors in the Hypothesis 29
        Strengths of the Hypothesis 34
        Weaknesses of the Hypothesis 38
        A "Sacrament of the Sacred" 39

Critical Questions and Decisions 41
    Decision 1: The Bible is a human product. 43
    Decision 2: Jesus is our authority. 43
    Critical Question 1: What is the nature of God? 44
    Critical Question 2: How does God interact with humanity? 48
    Critical Question 3: What does God expect of me? 61
    Decision 3: Accept Jesus' understanding of salvation 62
    Judgment and the "Faith vs. Works" Debate 65

Conclusion 69

Acknowledgments

Words cannot adequately express my appreciation to the many men and women who have been guiding lights on my Christian journey. I do want to acknowledge four very special people: Rev. George Haile, my pastor for 27 years, who was never afraid to address the hard questions and stand for Christian values; Dr. Glenn Hinson, who helped me balance the spiritual and intellectual sides of faith; and Dr. Marcus Borg, whose writing helped clarify my ideas about the Bible and the teachings of Jesus. Last, but certainly not least, I want to acknowledge my lovely wife, Patsy, who has encouraged me in this work, and who continues to inspire me by how she exhibits the Christian way with such ease and grace.

INTRODUCTION

I almost gave up on Christianity. Growing up in a conservative Protestant church, I was taught a lot of ideas about God, the Bible, salvation, and what was called faith. I never questioned most of this until I got older and began to really study the Bible. I slowly discovered that much of what I had been taught did not make sense in that it was internally inconsistent and sometimes contradictory. My childhood theology could not answer even the simplest questions about prayer or how to know what was authoritative.

I was taught that God loved the whole world, and yet this same God destroyed practically the whole world with a flood, sent a death angel to murder children, and commanded people to commit genocide. I was confused by the idea that the Bible is God's timeless truth. In one place eating shrimp and catfish was strictly forbidden, yet in other places it was fine. How can that be timeless truth?

Some passages seemed to be arbitrarily chosen to keep women subservient to men in church and in marriage. Sin was a big deal. Jesus' death was mentioned often, mostly as a payment to appease God's anger over all our sins. If this was the reason he died, how could Jesus have neglected to explain this to his followers, or did his disciples feel this was not important enough to record along with his other teachings?

Today, if a parent of three children arranged for one to be brutally murdered, and tried to justify this action by saying it was necessary to be able to love the other two, that parent should at least be locked away in an institution. Am I to believe that God's moral standards are less than what we would expect from a human parent?

Jesus taught that we should love our neighbors as ourselves. Was my church in the forefront of advocating for social justice? Sadly no, but it didn't really matter because all the church members believed they were saved regardless.

This version of Christianity just didn't make sense to me. I found it hard to believe that Jesus didn't teach a coherent understanding of the nature of God, how God interacts with us, and what God expects of us in this life.

When I asked for help in understanding these types of apparent conflicts, I was often told that I just had to accept everything on faith, that God's ways are not our ways. Some years later I read a story dating back to 1202 about a priest and a layman standing on a dock watching the ships come in. The layman said to the priest, "If the earth is flat like you teach, why is it that as the ship approaches the dock, I first see the top of the sail, then the deck and then the whole ship. If the earth is really flat, why don't I see all of the ship all the time?" The priest replied, "My son, there are just some things we will never understand."

I learned from this simple story that the premises or presuppositions or hypotheses we start with often limit the possible answers available for any question. A good hypothesis is validated by empirical data and leads to answers that are internally consistent and make sense.

In the physical world, there are many events and processes that cannot be established with absolute certainty. The Big Bang Theory, the theory of evolution, the age of the earth, and so on are hypotheses about how things happened based on the available empirical evidence. As the evidence changes, however, the hypotheses change to reflect the new information.

In the spiritual world, Christian church leaders have not been comfortable with uncertainty and have thus developed doctrines and creeds presented as absolute fact or truth. These doctrines are actually hypotheses taught as fact. Following are three examples.

First, the Catholic Church proposed, based on a particular interpretation of scripture, that the earth was at the center of the solar system and that the sun and stars rotated around the earth. This hypothesis was taught as fact until the empirical evidence to the contrary became so overwhelming that the church could no longer support it.

Second, the church hypothesized, based on a particular literal interpretation of the birth narratives in the gospels of Matthew and Luke, that Jesus' mother, Mary, was a virgin at his birth and remained so after his birth. This hypothesis, however, has strong evidence to the contrary found in scripture:

- The earliest gospel, Mark, makes no mention of an unusual birth of Jesus. It is hard to imagine how such an important event could have escaped his attention.

- The Apostle Paul, who wrote within a few decades of Jesus' death and years before the appearance of Mark's gospel, makes no mention of a miraculous birth. Paul even says that Jesus "descended from David according to the flesh," which means by a normal birth, and was "declared to be the Son of God . . . by resurrection from the dead" (Rom. 1:3-4).

- Mark's gospel also describes an event involving Jesus' family: "Then his mother and his brothers came; and standing outside, they sent to him (Jesus) and called him. A crowd was sitting around him; and they said to him, 'Your mother and your brothers and sisters are outside, asking for you'" (Mark 3:31-32). The writer of the earliest gospel seems to have had no problem with Jesus having brothers and sisters, which means Mary had other children.

- John's gospel makes no mention of the birth of Jesus. According to John, Jesus apparently descended to earth as a supernatural incarnation of God in adult human form.

Third, the Christian church—both Catholic and Protestant—has taught, based on a particular interpretation of scripture, mainly from the Hebrew Bible, that God interacts with humanity directly through rewards and punishments. As we shall see later, this idea is refuted by at least one book in the Hebrew Bible. Jesus actually challenged this hypothesis and offered a different way of understanding how God interacts with us, one that is actually supported by an abundance of empirical evidence.

As we seek to develop a coherent Christianity, we must understand that the historic creeds and doctrines widely accepted as fact in the past are actually just hypotheses. There are other interpretations of scripture that lead to other hypotheses that, for me, are much more meaningful and no less challenging.

The following diagram illustrates one "decision path" that, for me, has led to a coherent understanding of Christianity. This path, illustrated here with the key decision points (D1, D2, D3) shown, is based on the following idea.

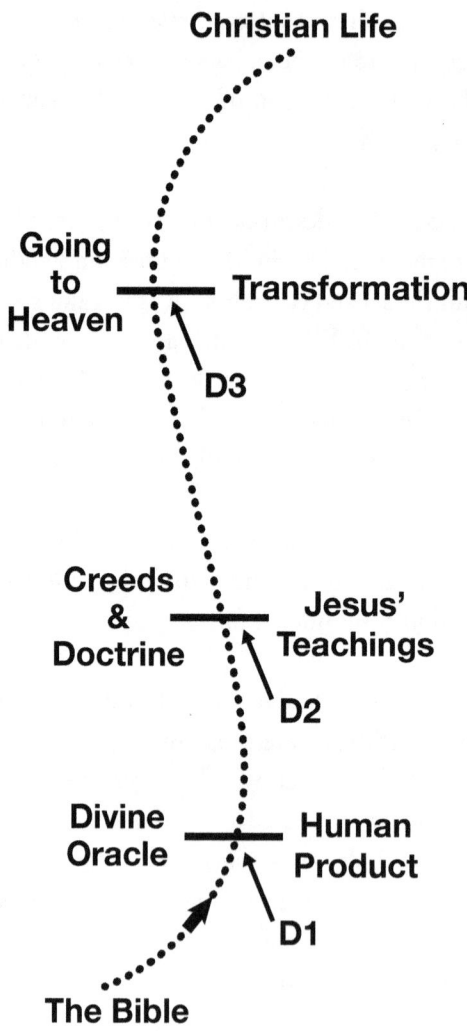

Suppose I had the opportunity to live under the direction of a very important and powerful person. The potential benefits are great, but there are also serious risks. What kind of questions would I have about this person? There are at least three critical ones.

First, what is the character of this person? More specifically, is he kind, patient, compassionate, honest, and forgiving *or* hateful, ill-tempered, and vengeful? If the answer is that the person is cruel and vengeful, I would relate to him out of fear but not love.

Second, how does this person interact with other people? Does she use coercion, rewards and punishments, and preferential treatment, or does she treat all people equally with dignity and respect? If this person acts capriciously and gives preferential treatment, I would try to placate any possible anger she would have and hopefully encourage favorable treatment. Many religious groups in the past developed sacrificial systems for this purpose.

The answers to these first two questions would shape my expectations of how this person might act toward me and respond to my requests for help.

Finally, what does this person expect of me? Is it possible for me to meet those expectations, and is this person going to help me succeed in meeting them?

Anyone contemplating a genuine personal relationship with and commitment to God should be able to find coherent answers to these critical questions. It makes sense to consider the following questions as they relate to the person of God:

1. What is the character of God?
2. How does God interact with humanity?
3. What does God expect of me?

The answer to each of these questions should complement the answers to the other ones. Our foundational and only significant document for answering these questions is the Bible.

SEEKING A NEW APPROACH TO COHERENT CHRISTIANITY

The available answers to the critical questions of our relationships with God depend to a large degree on how we understand the nature of the Bible. With the advent of modern biblical scholarship, there has been a continuing debate within the Christian community as to the nature of the Bible, its origin, and the nature of its authority. It is helpful to identify two hypotheses, one at either end of the debate.

1. The Bible is a divine oracle for which God is effectively the author.
2. The Bible is a human document, written by human hands under the direction of human minds sincere in their devotion to God.

In both cases, the general purpose of scripture is to instruct us about the nature of God and how God interacts with humanity. The choice of which way to view the Bible is decision 1 (D1). The second key choice is who or what within the Bible texts will be our authority in answering the three critical questions listed in the introduction (see p. 5). This is decision 2 (D2). The third key decision (D3) concerns the nature of salvation and the goal of a Christian life.

By making appropriate choices on our "path," we cannot only answer the critical questions above, but also develop a coherent understanding of Christianity and the Christian life.

THE BIBLE AS A DIVINE ORACLE: A HYPOTHESIS

The hypothesis of the Bible as a divine oracle claims that every word found in the Bible came directly from God. It is God's word or a collection of God's words, recorded by scribes without any deviation from God's intent. The writers were not required to be eyewitnesses to the events they recorded or to verify the authenticity of any of the events, such as the creation of the world in Genesis 1. The Bible is a monolithic block of divine given truth. If the Bible says it happened, it happened in the way described.

There are a number of consequences that follow from this hypothesis. For example, assuming that God's truth is timeless, the instructions given for righteous living are as true today as when first given. Based on the genealogies in Genesis 5 and 11, it is possible to calculate the approximate age of the earth to be approximately six thousand years old as done by Archbishop James Ussher (1581–1656). This view of the Bible is essential to those who define being a Christian as one who "believes" or professes the absolute truth of certain propositions extracted from scripture—for example, "Jesus died to save us from our sins." All required propositions must be believed because they are true, and they are true because they came from the Bible—which came directly from God.

Thinking of the Bible as a divine oracle is widely affirmed in conservative Christian churches, having received somewhat of a rebirth after Charles Darwin published *The Origin of Species* in 1859.

Factors in the Hypothesis

Any coherent understanding of what the Bible is and how it establishes standards for the Christian life involves three interrelated factors: origin, authority, and interpretation. The following approach is influenced by Marcus Borg's excellent book, *Reading the Bible Again for the First Time*.

Origin

According to Borg, "A divine oracle is a form of direct revelation, in which a divine being speaks to an individual without using an intermediary. The words of the oracle are the very words of the deity. Thus the scriptures, taken as a whole, are 'living oracles,' words of God that are perennially current, timeless in their significance."[1] Simply put, the Bible is a divine product, the Word of God, written by humans who were divinely inspired by the Holy Spirit and who wrote precisely as the Spirit directed.

Authority
Because its content comes from God, the Bible is true and must be the ultimate standard for belief and practice. All scripture must have equal authority since God is the author of the entire Bible. The term "inspiration" is often imputed to the texts and then used as proof of their divine origin and authority and guarantor of their truth.[2] Acknowledgment of the claims made on the reader still rests with the reader. (If the reader is coerced into giving assent to the claims, the authority becomes that of the person doing the coercing and not necessarily that of the Bible. Unfortunately, much of the brutality in church history is due to a failure to recognize this fact.)

Interpretation
Because its authority is based on God as the source, the contents must be factually and historically true, except when the text is obviously a parable or uses a metaphor such as "the trees of the field shall clap their hands" (Isa. 55:12). Otherwise, things actually happened as described. All scripture is equally true and authoritative, so interpretation of one text must never imply incorrectness of another. scripture must not contradict scripture.

Background of the Hypothesis

Prior to the Protestant Reformation the Catholic Church generally accepted the Bible as the "Word of God." The key concern was in regard to interpretation and the authority of the church to define the correct interpretation. The Bible and the Church shared authority in the sense that the United States Congress has the authority to write laws, but the courts have the authority to determine how the written laws are to be interpreted today and applied in real-life situations.

The call of the Protestant Reformation (1517–1648) for *sola scriptura* (scripture alone) emphasized the primacy of scripture over the Church's teachings. About 100 years after Martin Luther, reformation leaders began to use the terms "infallible" and "inerrant" to describe the Bible. Those later Reformation leaders emphasized plenary inspiration, or the notion that God dictated the words of the Bible and they are therefore free from error.[3]

In his 1874 publication of *Systematic Theology*, Charles Hodge, a Presbyterian minister and professor and principal (president) at Princeton Theological Seminary, published one of the foundational documents that reasserted the divine oracle hypothesis. Hodge based his understanding of the Bible in part on a portion of the Westminster Confession of 1646:

> The whole counsel of God concerning all things necessary for His own glory, man's salvation, faith, and life, is either expressly set down in scripture, or by good and necessary consequence may be deduced from scripture; unto which nothing at any time is to be added whether by new revelations of the Spirit or traditions of men.

From this statement and other parts of the Westminster Confession, Hodge listed three propositions Protestants should believe:[4]

> That the scriptures of the Old and New Testaments are the Word of God, written under the inspiration of the Holy Spirit, and are therefore infallible, and of divine authority in all things pertaining to faith and practice, and consequently free from all error whether of doctrine, fact, or precept.

> That they contain all the extant supernatural revelations of God designed to be a rule of faith and practice to his Church.

> That they are sufficiently perspicuous (clear and plain) to be understood by the people, in the use of ordinary means and by the aid of the Holy Spirit, in all things necessary to faith or practice, without the need of any infallible interpreter.

Hodge went on to discuss these propositions in greater detail. Regarding inspiration, he said that it was "an influence of the Holy Spirit on the minds of certain select men, which rendered them the organs of God for the infallible (incapable of error) communication of his mind and will. They were in such a sense the organs of God, that what they said God said."[5] In other words, according to Hodge, what is written in the Bible is exactly what God intended. So, when a prophet speaks or when a leader follows instructions from someone speaking on God's behalf, we are to trust that those instructions are indeed from God. Whatever the gospel writers wrote is to be considered as if it were direct from God, God's infallible word.

From this position it is a straightforward matter to conclude that: (a) *all* scripture is equally inspired, and (b) scripture can never contradict scripture. It must be harmonious, coherent, and free of any inconsistencies. Hodge stated, "If they (the scriptures) are a revelation from God, they must be received and obeyed; but they cannot be thus received without attributing to them divine authority, and they cannot have such authority without being infallible in all they teach."[6]

Princeton graduate Jack W. Cottrell, professor of theology at Cincinnati Christian University and a modern spokesman for this view of scripture, states:

> [T]he authority of the Bible is its right to compel belief and action (i.e., to establish norms of belief and conduct). The word "compel" is used in a moral sense only; it does not involve any kind of physical compulsion. Here it means "to persuade" or "to place under an obligation." The right to compel belief and action is not the same as the power to do so. When the Bible compels belief and action, it does so by right. We affirm the Bible's authority in this proper sense when we say that it alone is our rule of faith and practice.[7]

The Bible is authoritative because it is true, and it is true because it is God's infallible, inerrant Word. According to Cottrell, "Because it is God's revealed and inspired word, it *must* be inerrant, because an all-knowing and upright God could not and would not allow any errors, either deliberate or unintentional, to remain in the work to which he has given his stamp of approval. Thus 'God's Word' is by definition 'God's inerrant Word.'"[8]

Support for this view is found in the Bible in passages such as 2 Peter 2:21, ". . . because no prophecy ever came by human will, but men and women moved by the Holy Spirit spoke from God," and 2 Timothy 3:16, "All scripture is inspired (God-breathed) by God and is useful for teaching, for reproof, for correction, and for training in righteousness. . ."

Strengths of the Hypothesis

The idea of the Bible as divine oracle offers several strong points: It is simple and straightforward, offers a sense of security, and supports the notion that God is in control.

Simplicity

It is relatively easy to take the stories in the Bible literally. It does not require studying them in their historical context, which requires learning something of the political and religious conditions that existed at the time. Access to this type of knowledge was much more difficult to acquire in the past when few scholars published for lay people and there was no easy access to materials that are readily available today, especially on the internet. Also, believing that all of the Bible is God's word relieves the reader of the burden of trying to determine which text is most authoritative.

Security

Confidence in the scriptures has been a strong emphasis in many churches, especially in the Bible Belt. To paraphrase Charles Hodge, "What the Bible says, God says." Hence the popular saying, "The Bible says it; I believe it; that settles it." Since God's truth is timeless, instructions given in the Bible texts are reliable guides for life today, just as in the past. Hodge wrote: "The Bible is to the theologian what nature is to the man of science. It is his storehouse of facts."[9]

These "facts" must be stated as unambiguously as possible, so Bible "truths" are often stated in terms of objective propositions such as Jesus is the Son of God, Christ died on the cross as a propitiation for our sins, we are cleansed by the blood of Christ, the "Four Spiritual Laws," and so on. Having "faith" is often expressed in terms of belief in (giving intellectual assent to) these propositions. Professing assent to these propositions is often presented as a way to guarantee eternal security (salvation).

Sovereignty

Understanding the Bible as divine oracle also provides a way to understand it as an integrated whole, which shows God's will moving the course of history according to God's plan. Even though humanity may impede its progress, the course of history is assured by a sovereign God's divine intervention, as recorded in the great events of the Bible. God is in control. The Old Testament is seen as preparatory for the coming of the Christ, which, in turn, is preparatory to the end of the world and God's final judgment. In short, the Bible is salvation's history and promise of the future.

Weaknesses of the Hypothesis

The view of the Bible as divine oracle presents some serious problems to those who have a critical approach to any ancient text. Many of us have grown up in churches that adopted this view of scripture and could not or would not acknowledge these problems, much less try to address them. The divine oracle hypothesis denies that these problems exist, and some supporting arguments rely on questionable reasoning. The hypothesis also:

- denies evidence of inconsistencies in scripture
- cannot definitively answer critical questions
- often fails to honor historical context
- has led to a distortion of the meaning of faith
- often makes interpretation both critical and divisive
- denies primary authority to Jesus' teachings
- can border on idolatry
- offers great potential for abuse
- holds likely disillusionment

Questionable reasoning

One of the support arguments for the authority of scripture is as follows: (1) The Bible is authoritative because it is God's word, and (2) The Bible is God's word because it says it is. The proof text for this argument is typically 2 Timothy 3:16, "All scripture is inspired by God and is useful for teaching, for reproof, for correction, and for training in righteousness . . ." This argument is based on circular reasoning.

If a verse in the Koran said, "This was written by God," would a Christian feel compelled to believe that the Koran was as true as the Bible? Probably not. People who accept proof statements about the inspiration of the Bible have confidence in them because they have already decided to believe the Bible to be God's word. Also, at the time 2 Timothy was written, the New Testament, as we know it, did not exist.

Inconsistencies

C.H. Dodd said in 1929 that "any attempt to confront this theory of inspiration (dictation) with the actual facts which meet us in the study of the biblical documents leads at once to such patent confusions and contradictions that it is unprofitable to discuss it."[10] Modern scholarship has illuminated numerous inconsistencies in the scriptures both in the descriptions of identical events and in the descriptions of how God interacts with humanity. The following examples confirm that the proposition that scripture does not, and cannot, contradict scripture is not viable, and that therefore the Bible is neither inerrant nor infallible.

- There are two distinct accounts of the creation of the world in Genesis 1–2. The order of the creative activity is different. In the first account, men and women are created at the same time, after the animals, at the end of God's work. In the other account, man is created first, before the animals, after which woman is created. The two accounts even use different names for God, which suggests the stories come from different authors.

- We read in 2 Samuel 24:1, "Again the anger of the Lord was kindled against Israel, and he incited David against them, saying, 'Go, number Israel and Judah.'" However, in 1 Chronicles 21:1 the same event is described differently: "Satan stood up against Israel, and incited David to number Israel." In 2 Samuel the action is ascribed to God, but in 1 Chronicles it is attributed to Satan.

- Luke's version of Jesus' baptism is different from the story in Matthew where Jesus comes to be baptized by John. Luke does not say who baptizes Jesus, and in the verses prior to those describing the baptism Luke says that John is in prison.

- The gospels of Mark and John have Jesus being crucified on different days and at different times. According to Mark, Jesus takes the Passover meal with his disciples on the day the Passover lambs are sacrificed (14:12), that is, on Thursday evening. After this meal Jesus is arrested and taken to the high priest, then is held in jail overnight and taken to Pilate the next morning (15:1). Jesus is then crucified at 9 o'clock that morning, that is, on Friday (15:25). According to John's gospel, Jesus' trial takes place around noon on Thursday, the Day of Preparation for the Passover (19:14). Jesus is then crucified that afternoon. John is definite about the timing, saying that when the Jewish leaders take Jesus "from the high priest Caiaphas to Pilate's headquarters, they do not enter the headquarters, so as to avoid ritual defilement and to be able to eat the Passover" (18:28) meal, eaten on Thursday night.

- In the various gospels the accounts of the women visiting the tomb of Jesus cannot be reconciled. According to John, only Mary Magdalene goes to the tomb (20:1)). But in Matthew, Mary has another woman with her (28:1), and Luke has an indefinite number (24:10). Luke tells us the women return to tell the disciples, but Mark says they flee from the tomb, "for terror and amazement had seized them; and they said nothing to anyone, for they were afraid" (16:8). The book, *Gospel Parallels: A Comparison of the Synoptic Gospels*,[11] confirms that the synoptic gospel writers differed in their versions of many events in the life of Jesus.

- William Barclay points out that in Mark's gospel the author has Jesus "remind the Pharisees of what David did in the days of Abiathar the high priest" (Mark 2:26). Both Matthew and Luke omit the priest's name (Matt. 12:1-8, Luke 6:1-5). The priest in question is not Abiathar, but rather his son Ahimelech (1 Sam. 21:1-6, 2 Sam. 8:17). In the same discussion Barclay points out Paul's two very different opinions of marriage (1 Corinthians 7, Ephesians 5) and notes that Paul confesses in one letter that what he is writing is not from the Lord, but is only his opinion (1 Cor. 7:12, 25).[12]

- The prophet Nahum has God say of Nineveh, capital of Assyria: "I am against you, says the Lord of hosts, and will lift up your skirts over your face; and I will let nations look on your nakedness and kingdoms on your shame. I will throw filth at you and treat you with contempt, and make you a spectacle" (Nahum 3:5-7). Yet we find in the book of Jonah that God has great compassion for the people of Nineveh and sends Jonah to tell them of God's care for them. Thus the scripture says that God is against Nineveh some of the time and for Nineveh at other times.

- The prophet Elisha sends a member of the company of prophets to anoint Jehu as God's elect to destroy the house of Ahab in the northern territory of Israel. Elisha proclaims, "Thus says the Lord God of Israel: I anoint you king over the people of the Lord, over Israel. You shall strike down the house of your master Ahab, so that I may avenge on Jezebel the blood of my servants the prophets and the blood of all the servants of the Lord" (2 Kgs. 9:7). Later, Hosea condemns the terrible atrocities that brought Jehu to power: "And the Lord said to him, . . . in a little while I will punish the house of Jehu for the blood of Jezreel, and I will put an end to the kingdom of the house of Israel" (1:4). Are we to believe that God deliberately brought Jehu to power without knowing what type of person he was or that God didn't care about the atrocities he would commit? Did God deliberately choose such a bad person? Are we to believe that in order to punish Jehu, God brought down the whole nation of Israel and thereby caused the suffering of many innocent people—even though God caused Jehu to be in power in the first place?

- In 2 Samuel 24 God incites David to take a census. Later, David considers this census such a grave sin that he deserves punishment. Instead of punishing David directly, however, God sends a terrible plague so that 70,000 innocent people die (24:15). Such a punishment inflicted on the people who had no control over ordering the census is unjust in the extreme. This conflicts with many of the prophets' and Jesus' portrayal of God as perfect love, one who desires justice and mercy, especially for the innocent and the disadvantaged.

Critical questions

In addition to the conflicts and inconsistencies noted above, there are other conflicting passages regarding the character of God, how God interacts with humanity, and what God expects for us to have a successful relationship with him.

- In Matthew 5:48 Jesus says, "Be perfect, therefore, as your heavenly Father is perfect." How are we to understand what "perfect" means? Jesus shows God as gracious and forgiving in the parable of the loving father (or prodigal son). At the beginning of John's gospel we find "For God so loved the world . . ." Jesus taught, "But I say to you, Love your enemies and pray for those who persecute you so that you may be children of your Father in heaven" (Matt. 5:44-45a). If unselfish, self-giving love is what characterizes God, consider the sharp contrast with the character of God presented in parts of the Hebrew Bible where God destroys the world in anger, brings plagues on the Egyptians, sends a death angel to murder children and babies, and deploys pagan armies to destroy the righteous and unrighteous among God's chosen people.

- In the promise of unlimited retribution, God said that later generations would be punished for the sins of earlier generations (see Exod. 20:1-6). Just prior to the destruction of the Temple (587 BCE), some prophets recognized the injustice of this doctrine. While Jeremiah addressed this to some extent (31:29-30), Ezekiel was the most vocal on the subject (ch. 18, esp. vv. 1-4). The promise of unlimited retribution was expressed by the popular expression, "The parents have eaten sour grapes, and the children's teeth are set on edge." According to Ezekiel, God rejected this notion and said that each person is responsible for his/her actions (18:20), thus contradicting the promise given in Exodus 20.

- In the Hebrew Bible, God deals coercively with humanity through rewards and punishments—as noted in the Covenant (see Deuteronomy 28). This shows God giving preferential treatment based on faithfulness to the Covenant. Jesus said that God "makes his sun rise on the evil and on the good, and sends rain on the righteous and on the unrighteous" (Matt. 5:45). In the parable of the prodigal son, Jesus pictures the father as never acting in a coercive way toward either of his sons but rather loving them unconditionally. Jesus calls us to this type of unselfish, self-giving, non-coercive love. Thus the Bible gives conflicting views of whether or not God is coercive. These are fundamentally different and mutually exclusive ways of understanding how God deals with humanity, unless one believes that God's method of dealing with humanity and God's moral values change with time. But, if that is true, how are we to understand the psalmist's declaration, "Praise the LORD! O give thanks to the LORD, for he is good; for his steadfast love endures forever" (Ps. 106:1)? How are we to talk of God-given moral principles if God's moral values change with time?

- The Hebrew Bible contains numerous laws (Leviticus 11) regarding what is proper to eat and what is prohibited. Obedience to these laws was seen as important behavior in maintaining a proper relationship with God. Jesus declared that these laws were not the will of God, however. "It is not what goes into the mouth that defiles a person, but it is what comes out of the mouth that defiles" (Matt. 15:11). Jesus clearly contradicted what was understood in his day to be God's specific instructions.

Historical context

The publication of Darwin's *Origin of Species* on November 22, 1859 created a storm of controversy because it appeared to refute the biblical creation accounts. Science had called into question the validity and trustworthiness of the Bible. In response, the conservative religious community appealed to their own "facts" found in the Bible. For these "facts" to have equal authority to those proposed by science, the source of these religious "facts" must be absolutely true and trustworthy. It is no coincidence that fifteen years after *Origin of Species*, Charles Hodge would write, "The Bible is to the theologian what nature is to the man of science. It is his storehouse of facts."[13]

The effect of thinking of the Bible as the religious equivalent of a scientific document has often had the effect of limiting the bounds of interpretation so that the literal interpretation is seen as the only valid one or at least the preferred one. This can rob the Bible of much of its beauty and its ability to mediate the presence of God to the reader.

The Bible is written using many literary styles such as historical narratives, metaphor, poetry, and symbolic language. Many scholars suggest that the ancient eastern mind was very comfortable with symbolic language and metaphor. To force biblical stories to conform to a modern scientific epistemology is to dishonor the work of the biblical writers and perhaps to distort the original meaning of the text by not allowing it to speak from its own historical context. The effect is that when one encounters a biblical story of the miraculous or an apparently unscientific description of an event, the key question often becomes, "Is this story really true?" rather than, "What does this story mean and how does it serve the author's purpose in its original setting?"

The notion of inerrancy and infallibility carries with it the idea that words found in the Bible are timeless. Because it is God's truth, what was spoken in the past has equal authority for us today. The command that women be silent in church (1 Cor. 14:34-35) was written in a specific time in response to a specific problem in a specific church. The notion of inerrancy means that command is God's word and is therefore binding on churches today since there is no text that specifically puts time limits on its authority. When scripture tells slaves to submit themselves to their masters, does this imply that God sees slavery as legitimate? Some early Christian churches had their members sell all their possessions and live communally with all things held in common. Is that a good model for us today? The notion of inerrancy and infallibility gives no clear guidelines on when it is appropriate to impose practices, rules, or commands given nearly two thousand years ago on our present-day communities.

Faith

Seeing the Bible as divine oracle has historically led to the formation of creeds and doctrines, which are statements of important propositional truths of scripture. "Faith" has often been equated to professing assent to these statements. The necessity of inerrancy to the understanding of faith as assent to propositional truths is stated clearly by Sandra Schneiders, now professor emerita in the Jesuit School of Theology at the Graduate Theological Union in Berkeley, California:

> Infallibility and inerrancy as essential notes of scripture are integral to a fundamentalistic position that understands scripture to have originated miraculously (e.g., by divine dictation or verbal inspiration) and therefore to contain propositional revelation that makes an absolutely authoritative claim upon and constitutes the unique and absolute norm of faith. The importance of inerrancy of the text in such a theology of scripture derives from the latter's conception of revelation as propositional. If propositions are to be authoritative, they must be true, and if they are to be absolutely authoritative, they must be absolutely true. If some propositions in scripture are false or mistaken, then, in principle, any or all could be, and the ground of faith would be destroyed. Hence the importance of maintaining the infallibility of the authors. They did not err because they could not err; therefore, all the propositions in the Bible are true (inerrant), authoritative, and normative.[14]

Defining "faith" as "assent to a list of propositions" has led to a terrible distortion of the original meaning of faith, which was trust. For example, believing in the proposition that Jesus was the Son of God is not the same as trusting that Jesus' teachings are our standards for behavior. Jesus said we should visit people in prison, help the weak and vulnerable, love mercy, show compassion, be willing to forgive, resist being judgmental, and be passionate about seeking equal justice and opportunities for everyone. According to the account of Jesus' temptation given in Luke 4, even the devil believed Jesus was the Son of God. Those church leaders who led the Inquisition; burned Jews, heretics, and others at the stake; tortured and killed those who expressed a different interpretation of scripture: all readily professed complete acceptance of the church's propositions *about* Jesus and their plan of salvation.

Faith originally meant trust in the truth of Jesus' message. When Jesus said to the woman with the issue of blood, "Your faith has made you well," he was not talking about her having pledged allegiance to a set of propositions about him (see Mark 5:25-34). When Jesus encountered the centurion who asked him to heal the servant without actually seeing the servant, Jesus said, "Truly I tell you, in no one in Israel have I found such faith" (see Matt. 8:5-13). When Jesus healed blind Bartimaeus he told him, "Go; your faith has made you well" (see Mark 10:46-52). When Jesus stilled a storm he said to his disciples, "Why are you afraid? Have you still no faith?" (see Mark 4:35-41). Was Jesus asking if his disciples had pledged allegiance to some set of propositional statements about him?

Of course, Jesus was not thinking of faith in that way, in the way it is commonly used today. Since Jesus taught and ministered, our definition of the word "faith" has changed drastically. In his time, faith meant "trust." Jesus said to the woman who had the issue of blood, "Because you trusted me to have the power to heal you, you have been healed." He said to the centurion, "Because you trusted me to have the power to heal and have compassion on your servant, your servant has been healed." Using the concept of an infallible scripture that leads to "faith" as assent to some inerrant propositions distorts the original meaning and is often used as an alternative to Jesus' call to be his followers by living according to the principles he taught.

Interpretation

The ideas of inerrancy and infallibility carry with them the notion that there is a "right" interpretation for any text. If this were not so, it might imply that God was intentionally ambiguous in transmitting the intent of that text to the biblical writer. If there are two or more equally valid ways of interpreting a given text, then the notion of inerrancy becomes very nebulous. When there are contradictions, can the Bible be a dependable source of "facts"? Who decides what interpretation is the one God intended and thus the one the community will pass on to future generations as "truth"?

Someone or some group must assume this responsibility and thus assume the authority to know the mind of God. A situation is then created in which one or more fallible people assume responsibility to discern and control the infallible truth contained in God's Word. In the words of Charles Hodge,

> If the scriptures be a plain book, and the Spirit performs the functions of a teacher to all the children of God, it follows inevitably that they must agree in all essential matters in their interpretation of the Bible. And from that fact it follows that for an individual Christian to dissent from the faith of the universal Church (i.e., the body of true believers), is tantamount to dissenting from the scriptures themselves.[15]

The history of the New Testament church shows that, even with the help of the Holy Spirit, the leaders of the church who have assumed the power to interpret the scripture for others have used it badly. Prior to the Reformation, people who espoused unorthodox interpretations were labeled heretics and many were burned at the stake, in spite of clear commands in God's Word to love your neighbor and treat others the way you would want to be treated. The Reformation happened because of a difference in interpretation of scripture. The Protestant movement itself split numerous times because of differences in interpretation.

In the twentieth century the controversy over interpretation caused much division within mainline denominations. In Southern Baptist life it was common to hear the charge, "If you don't interpret the Bible the way I do, you don't believe the Bible." In other words, "There are many ways to interpret scripture, but my way is the only right way. I know what the Bible says and what it means." This attitude is illustrated by a conversation between journalist-commentator Bill Moyers and W.A. Criswell, long-time pastor of First Baptist Church in Dallas, Texas, aired on public television around 1987. Moyers asked Criswell about the Baptist tradition of the right to private interpretation of scripture. Criswell replied that if anyone would allow themselves to be truly led by the Holy Spirit, they would come to the same interpretation as his own.[16] Such a mentality in Southern Baptist life has led to an "us versus them" attitude in which anyone who disagrees with those in power are systematically excluded from the denomination's institutions and fellowship. Glenn Hinson, a well-known author and professor who was excluded from a Southern Baptist seminary controlled by those with attitudes similar to those of Criswell, has said he finds it hard to believe that God's power to illuminate is of such low "wattage" that it only reaches a chosen few.

Authority

Viewing scripture as divine oracle maintains that *all* scripture is the Word of God. It is all equally authoritative. The Bible is one monolithic block of truth, direct from God. This means that the words spoken by the prophets regarding what God said or did are equally authoritative to those of Jesus. It also follows that the teachings of Paul are equally authoritative with the teachings of Jesus. Yet, at the same time, many Christians who hold this view profess that Jesus is Lord and Savior, God's ultimate revelation to humanity. It is at least disingenuous to proclaim Jesus as Lord and God incarnate and not give priority to his teachings.

In Mark's account of the transfiguration (also found in Matt. 17:1-8 and Luke 9:28-36), Jesus appears with Elijah and Moses, and we read, "Then a cloud overshadowed them, and from the cloud there came a voice, 'This is my Son, the Beloved; listen to him!'" (Mark 9:7). The voice did not say, "listen to Jesus and Moses and Elijah." It said listen to Jesus. If these are indeed the words of God, shouldn't this imply that what Jesus taught should have precedence over anything else?

One example of how the priority of Jesus' teachings has been suppressed is the way women's opportunities to serve in leadership roles in some churches have been limited. Jesus taught us to "do unto others as you would have them do unto you," which can be interpreted to mean that in God's kingdom women should be given the same opportunities to serve as men, especially in the church. In some writings attributed to Paul, women are admonished to be silent in church (1 Cor. 14:34). With few exceptions, throughout its history the Christian church has arbitrarily chosen Paul's words over those of Jesus. Other texts in the Bible have been used by supposedly Christian communities to justify slavery, social injustice, and all types of persecution of people both inside and outside the church—all in opposition to the direct teachings of Jesus to love your neighbor and treat others as you would like to be treated.

The primary consequence of denying that Jesus' teachings have final authority is that without that final authority it is not possible to resolve the contradictions in scripture with regard to the nature of God and how God deals with humanity. I believe that not being able to resolve these contradictions is a significant reason many people have simply given up on Christianity.

Idolatry

When interpretation of scripture becomes fixed, doctrine becomes fixed. As stated in the Westminster Confession, everything necessary "is expressly set down in scripture, or . . . may be deduced from scripture; unto which nothing at any time is to be added whether by new revelation of the Spirit or traditions of men." This comes close to making the Bible a substitute for God.

There is an interesting story in Exodus 32 about Aaron building a golden calf while Moses was on the mountain communing with God. Contrary to popular opinion, the calf was not a false god, but rather an image representing the God who had brought the Hebrews out of Egypt. The Hebrews wanted security, something they could see and touch, something "real." The divine oracle approach to the Bible is in danger of making the Bible another golden calf. At the very least, it seems to put God and the Holy Spirit in a static box in the sense that God has nothing new to communicate. To equate the authority of the Bible with the authority of God is to fall into the sin of idolatry.[17]

Abuse

Considering the Bible infallible and inerrant makes it a monolithic block of truth. The history of the church shows that there is an almost irresistible temptation to pick and choose passages that support those in power at the expense of the less powerful. The Bible has been used to justify the divine right of kings, slavery, marginalization of women, social injustice, even torture and murder. This has been easily accomplished by selecting certain passages to create a doctrine whose acceptance is mandatory. To be against that doctrine was to be against the Bible, and thus anti-God. This allowed the teachings of Jesus to be superseded by doctrine and those anti-God heretics to be punished or killed. The Nicene Creed was worded specifically to exclude people who claimed to be Christians but had a different interpretation of scripture.

Disillusionment

The divine oracle view can be maintained by hiding the difficulties in scripture and by suppressing inquiry. Many young people who eventually move away from their sheltered communities often encounter people of other religions or even other Christians who do not regard the Bible as a divine oracle. When the difficulties noted above are pointed out to them, confidence in the integrity of the Bible can be severely damaged. If they have no other way of understanding the Bible, they often abandon Christianity.

A "House of Cards"

At the beginning of this discussion, I presented three critical questions:

1. What is the character of God?
2. How does God interact with humanity?
3. What does God expect of me?

Viewing the Bible as a divine product, effectively written by God and containing God's timeless truth—all with equal authority—does not permit definitive answers to these critical questions because there are passages in scripture that give conflicting answers.

The attributes of inerrancy and infallibility have the unfortunate effect of making the divine oracle view of scripture somewhat like a house of cards. If inerrancy and infallibility cannot be maintained absolutely, then this whole system falls. Infallibility requires that scripture cannot contradict scripture. Numerous examples have been given where scripture does indeed contradict scripture. Internal evidence does not support infallibility. If infallibility is not supported, then God's sole authorship is not supported. Thus the divine oracle hypothesis fails as a coherent way to understand the nature of scripture.

These difficulties do not mean that scripture is without authority, or that it was not written by people who were devoted to God, or that it is unable to contribute in a powerful way to our relationship with God and our neighbors. The divine oracle hypothesis is *one way* to understand scripture. The next section presents a different way. This new way allows scripture to speak both in the past and in our day. It does not limit the Holy Spirit from playing an active and ongoing role in our interpretation of scripture. This new way gives priority to Jesus' teachings and does not define "faith" in terms of propositional statements *about* Jesus.

Notes

[1] Carl R. Holladay, "Contemporary Methods of Reading the Bible" in *The New Interpreter's Bible*, ed. L.E. Keck (Nashville: Abingdon, 1994) I: 125-149.

[2] Phyllis A. Bird, "The Authority of the Bible," in *The New Interpreter's Bible*, ed. L.E. Keck (Nashville: Abingdon, 1994) I:35.

[3] Marcus Borg, *Reading the Bible Again for the First Time* (New York: Harper Collins, 2001), 7.

[4] Charles Hodge, *Systematic Theology*, vol.1 (New York: Scribner, Armstrong and Co., 1874), 152; accessed at https://www.ccel.org/ccel/hodge/theology1.

[5] Ibid., 154.

[6] Ibid., 166.

[7] Jack. W. Cottrell, "The Nature of Biblical Authority: A Conservative Perspective," *Conservative Moderate Liberal: The Biblical Authority Debate*, ed. Charles R. Blaisdell (St. Louis: CBP Press, 1990), 23.

[8] Ibid., 29.

[9] Hodge, *Systematic Theology*, 10.

[10] C.H. Dodd, *The Authority of the Bible* (New York: Harper & Brothers, 1929), 35.

[11] Burton H. Throckmorton Jr., *Gospel Parallels: A Comparison of the Synoptic Gospels* (Nashville: Thomas Nelson, 1992).

[12] William Barclay, *Introducing the Bible* (Nashville: Abingdon, 1972), 141-143.

[13] Hodge, *Systematic Theology*, 10.

[14] Sandra Schneiders, *The Revelatory Text* (Collegeville, MN: Liturgical Press, 1999), 54.

[15] Hodge, *Systematic Theology*, 184.

[16] Bill Moyers, "A Second Look: The Battle for the Bible," in *God and Politics* series, aired May 21, 1989, billmoyers.com.

[17] Bird, *The New Interpreter's Bible*, 36.

THE BIBLE AS A COLLECTION OF HUMAN DOCUMENTS: A HYPOTHESIS

An alternative to the divine oracle hypothesis is that which views the Bible as a collection, or library, of human documents written over many centuries, under different cultural circumstances, and to varied audiences. While the writers shared a common purpose to enlighten their readers and hearers, they freely wrote from their own cultural and religious perspectives, each influenced by his religious training and personal encounters with God. Each brought his own theological interpretation of historical events.

Viewing the Bible as a collection of human documents does not deny God's influence on the writers, but maintains that this influence was not coercive. The term "God's influence" is used rather than "inspiration" because inspiration has no universally accepted definition. This second hypothesis regarding how scripture came into being heartily supports the idea that the writers were acting under their conviction of the presence of God in their history, in their current situations, and in their future.

This hypothesis sees the Bible as our sacred text, sacred in function but not of divine origin. A sacred text is one worthy of veneration, reverence, and respect. We often see ourselves in the people of the scriptures and their situations. We see how others discerned God's influence in their lives and how they lived out their devotion to God. The Bible provides the theological basis for our own relationship to God. We see Jesus' life and ministry in the context of centuries of religious thought, the traditions Jesus honored and those he rejected. The Bible is our "lens" through which we perceive the nature of God and our relationship with God. Through this lens we learn to worship God and not the lens.[1] We honor and pay respect to all scripture for its teaching and guiding function, even though we may not assign to all of it equal authority.

The abundance of internal evidence in the Bible suggests that its books are products of the faith of the various writers who documented their understanding of God and how God interacts with humanity. These books reflect both theological views and cultural influences that have changed over time. They were written by people deeply devoted to God and to passing on their theological knowledge and understanding to future generations.

Factors in the Hypothesis

As in the analysis of the divine oracle hypothesis, in examining the Bible as a collection of human documents, we consider three critical factors that help define this alternative way of understanding the Bible: origin, authority, and interpretation. Note that each of these factors in this hypothesis is dramatically different from the corresponding factor in the divine oracle hypothesis.

Origin

The books of the Bible are human products. The Bible is a library, a collection of human documents, each written by its author or authors out of sincere devotion to God and a genuine desire to document the "truth" as the author understood it for the benefit of the intended audience.

Authority

Authority means the power to affect behavior. Seeing the Bible as a collection or library of human documents means that its authority derives from the consent of the reader. In the introductory material of the 1994 *New Interpreter's Bible*, the section on the nature of authority contains the following:

> Debates over biblical authority tend to focus on particular attributes of the text and neglect the fundamentally relational character of all authority. Authority describes the power of one subject to influence another in such a way that a claim upon the other is established and acknowledged. The nature of the claim and the manner of its operation will vary with the subject and the relationship in which it is exercised, but it is not effected by assertion alone; it requires acknowledgment—through appropriate response. Authority is not a possession, nor can it be freely created. It is a quality of a relationship that develops over time and involves an element of trust and trustworthiness. And it is always exercised within a community.[2]

In this understanding, all scripture does not necessarily have equal authority, since authority depends on the consent of the reader to acknowledge its claims and a choice to be guided by its teachings. For example, Christians need not feel bound to obey the kosher food laws found in the Hebrew Bible, as Jesus taught his followers not to feel bound by them (Matt. 15:10-20, Mark 7:14-23).

Interpretation

In approaching the Bible as a collection of human documents, there are three guiding principles for interpretation of scripture. I am especially indebted to Marcus Borg for the first two.

1. We must always seek to understand a story or passage in its historical context before applying it in today's situation. We must first seek to learn what the story or passage might have meant to the original hearers. The biblical writers always sought to convey "truth" as they understood it. The means to convey that truth took many forms, including story, metaphor, parable, etc. The teaching function of story can be seen in the text itself:

   - "And when your children say to you, 'What do you mean by this service?' you shall say . . ." (Exod. 12:26)
   - "And when in time your son asks you, 'What does this mean?' you shall say to him . . ." (Exod. 13:14)
   - "When your son asks you in time to come, 'What is the meaning of the testimonies and the statutes and the ordinances which the Lord our God has commanded you?' Then you shall say to your son . . ." (Deut. 6:20-21).[3]

   The primary information to be conveyed was about meaning, and the meaning contained in the story was far more important than the factual accuracy of the story.

   We live in a period of Western cultural history known by philosophers as modernity. It began with the Enlightenment of the seventeenth century and is unique in history in large measure because of the rise of the scientific method of investigation. Today, when most people speak of knowing something is true, they mean it is true because it can be verified by experimentation, or it is a hypothesis that has such an abundance of evidence to support it that a reasonable person would find it difficult not to accept it as true.

For most of us today, to talk about "truth" or to say something is "true" is not only to say *what* we know is true, but also *how* we know it is true. Truth in this modern way of thinking implies authority in that it makes a claim and demands acknowledgment. To deny the claim is to deny the evidence that supports the claim. To deny the evidence, we would need to find opposing evidence or facts that refute the claim. It is no coincidence that Charles Hodge would see the Bible as a storehouse of facts with which he could refute the "truth" implied by Darwin's *Origin of Species*.

The contributors of the various stories in the Bible obviously lived in very different times and therefore understood truth in a different way. They took for granted that there were supernatural forces at work controlling history and the physical world. Whether the sun revolved around the earth or vice versa was not a pressing issue. The cyclical rising and setting of the sun on a regular schedule was vitally important. It was therefore prudent to know something about the supernatural forces that controlled the sun and not do anything that might jeopardize this regularity. How the water got into the sky was also not a pressing problem for the biblical writer's mind. That the water came down at the right time was critical, as were planting and harvesting at the right times.

Because they believed God controlled nature as well as historical events, this method of interpretation takes the position that the primary goal of the writers of our biblical texts was not historical or scientific factual accuracy but, rather, illumination of what they believed to be theological truth. It was important to know something about the principles by which God interacted with humanity and what God expected of them.

Therefore, for the biblical writer, truth is that which served as a reliable or dependable standard, rule, or guide for belief or practice in relation to God. Something was true when it taught, defined, or illuminated truth in relation to God. In this sense, the biblical stories were true for their writers because they conveyed what the writers believed to be truth for life under God, regardless of whether the stories were factually true. This does not imply that the writers ever wrote to deceive their readers, but that the theological and spiritual truths being conveyed were much more important than the factual accuracy of the stories.

2   The second principle of interpretation in this hypothesis is that it uses a metaphorical approach to the text. It understands that much of the biblical text is history-metaphorized: It is history remembered and recorded in story form so as to use stories as vehicles or lenses that enable the reader to "see" particular interpretations of history and learn the theological truths conveyed in those stories. We study the text anticipating that the author had, where possible, mixed history and metaphor. We hope to find the original meaning contained in the historical metaphor, but not be limited by it. This approach "enables us to see and affirm meanings that go beyond the particularity of what the texts meant in their ancient setting."[4]

Seeing a text as metaphorical language allows for more than one meaning and thus more than one possibility for illumination. When is it appropriate to apply the metaphorical approach? In the case of historical narratives, stories that make use of rich symbolic motifs that allude to other historical figures or events are good candidates for this approach. In the case of spectacular events such as walking on water or living three days in the belly of a fish, one might ask whether such events have ever happened to anyone else anywhere or anytime since the initial event report. If the answer is no, then the story is a good candidate for the metaphorical approach.

The historical-metaphorical approach to scripture allows meanings to be discovered that are not limited to the past. As Borg notes, "Finally, metaphors can be profoundly true, even though they are not literally true. Metaphor is poetry plus, not factuality minus. That is, metaphor is not less than fact, but more. Some things are best expressed in metaphorical language; others can be expressed only in metaphorical language."⁵

3 The third principle of interpretation in this model is that scripture presents a story of a progressive discovery of the nature of God and how God interacts with humanity. For the Christian, Jesus provides the best and fullest illumination in this discovery process. This is consistent with the concept of authority outlined above. Note that this principle is not the same as "progressive revelation" whereby God's revelation is different over time and culturally conditioned. Progressive discovery says that God has been trying to communicate the same message, namely God's will for humanity, consistently over time and that humanity has slowly been discovering and clarifying the content of that message.

An excellent summary of this idea of progressive discovery is given by Harry Emerson Fosdick in his book, *A Guide to Understanding the Bible*. Fosdick contrasts some of the ideas of God early in Hebrew history with those found in the New Testament writings. Early ideas of God included God walking in the garden (Genesis 3), a storm God who resided on a mountain, a God so terrifying that hearing his voice could bring death (Deuteronomy 5), and a God who murders babies and children (Exodus 12). Following Jesus' life and resurrection, we find very different ideas: God is love, and God is Spirit (John 4); God is the one in whom we live and move and have our being (Acts 17); God wills that not one of these little ones should perish (Matthew 18).⁶

In between these early and late understandings of God are the voices of the prophets and writers who perceived in God a desire for justice, compassion, peace, and mercy. Some envisioned a God who doesn't use rewards and punishments (Book of Job) or punish children for the sins of their parents (Jeremiah). While God's character has remained consistent over time, our discovery of God's nature has progressed with Jesus giving us the most complete revelation of all. We should not denigrate the earlier writers, but rather appreciate their contributions to this progressive discovery process.

Strengths of the Hypothesis

Viewing the Bible as a collection of human documents acknowledges two types of truth, honors both scientific and spiritual or moral truth, honors biblical scholarship, recognizes cultural differences, addresses inconsistencies, deals with both faith and authority, and opens the way for new perspectives in study.

Truth

This approach to understanding the Bible recognizes that there is scientific truth and spiritual or moral truth. Scientific truths (facts in today's language) are what can be known through the scientific method, that is, what can be verified or proven by repeatable procedures, or for which there is enough evidence to support the validity of a hypothesis about the reality of something.

There are also spiritual ideas that we accept as true because they come from a source to which we have given authority. For example, Jesus taught that God's will was encapsulated in the Great Commandment to love God and neighbor. If we accept this as true, it is because of the authority we have given to Jesus' teachings. It is a truth not verifiable by the scientific method. Many Christians believe that all truth, scientific or otherwise, comes from God, which is also a spiritual truth not verifiable by the scientific method.

It is important to distinguish between these two types of truth. The church has a bad history of using the Bible to extract "scientific" information such as the operation of the solar system or the age of the earth. When the church has been proven wrong, this has hurt its credibility to speak to spiritual issues. Seeing the Bible as a collection of human documents written in the past, before the age of scientific inquiry, helps to focus attention on the stories in the Bible to discover their spiritual truths and interpret these stories as described above. Spiritual truth and scientific truth need never be in conflict.

Biblical scholarship

Today we are able to take advantage of more than a hundred years of good biblical scholarship. The scriptures have been analyzed using modern techniques that have been applied to other types of literature. Scholars who understand the languages in which the biblical texts were written are able to recognize word patterns and writing styles and can identify different individual contributors even in a single book. These scholars are often able to date when a story was written by its style and references to known historical events and people, and thus gain important insights into the political and spiritual contexts of the story. It is also possible to recognize individual story units and how they have been intentionally combined into a larger story.

The Bible is written in both prose and poetry, historical narrative, metaphor, and parable. The larger story is made up of many smaller stories contained in the various books. This scholarship reveals the inconsistencies and illuminates the uniqueness of the various stories and books.

Cultural differences

The principles of interpretation in this method require that we seek to understand scriptural passages in their historical context and recognize that our view of the world is vastly different from that of the biblical writers. We must first seek the historical meaning in the historical context. This enables us to see meanings "that otherwise would remain buried in the past"[7] and also helps us determine the applicability of the story for us today.

Inconsistencies

In viewing the scriptures as a collection of human documents, each book of the Bible reflects the understanding of the writer or writers and their own concepts of the nature of God and how God deals with humanity. Each writer brings a unique perspective and has a unique objective for his book. Thus, the fact that there are inconsistencies is not a problem but a strength since this gives us multiple sources from which to understand the historical context and the theological perspective of that writer at that time.

Inconsistencies are to be expected, not feared. We know that the various books of the Bible were written only after periods of oral tradition, and thus are mixtures of remembrances of past events and interpretations of those events. Interpretation was always influenced by the religious and social conditions at the time of writing. We also know that many of the books, particularly in the Hebrew Bible (Old Testament), are compilations of different traditions and that many have been redacted over time so that the final form reflects the redactor's goals and religious context.

For example, the stories of the Exodus and the conquest of Canaan show God directly or indirectly involved in terrible acts of violence against others. Such acts are inconsistent with the compassionate, merciful God that Jesus taught. The older ideas of a God capable of violence simply reflect the theology and culture of that time, a theology not unlike that of all the other nations. We acknowledge these ideas in their historical context, but they do not define God for us today. We are not bound by these older ideas.

Faith and authority

When the Bible is seen as a collection of human documents, then the issue of authority is critical. All passages do not necessarily have the same authority. The critical question is what parts of scripture have ultimate authority, or which parts express the best and most complete revelation of God's will and truth for us. For someone who claims to be a Christian, a follower of Jesus, the answer must be obvious. The teachings of Jesus, by both word and deed, must be our final authority on the nature of God, how God deals with humanity, God's will, and how we should behave. The word "faith" now recovers its original meaning, that of "trust" in Jesus and his teachings; trust that is demonstrated by the way we live rather than profession of assent to propositional statements and doctrines about Jesus.

New perspectives

Viewing the Bible as documents written by human hands allows new perspectives in interpretation. Consider the passage from 1 Timothy 2:9-15 regarding women in the church:

> [W]omen should dress themselves modestly and decently in suitable clothing, not with their hair braided, or with gold, pearls, or expensive clothes, but with good works, as is proper for women who profess reverence for God. Let a woman learn in silence with full submission. I permit no woman to teach or to have authority over a man; she is to keep silent. For Adam was formed first, then Eve; and Adam was not deceived, but the woman was deceived and became a transgressor. Yet she will be saved through childbearing, provided they continue in faith and love and holiness, with modesty.

When the Bible is seen as a divine oracle, this passage is God's direct command regarding women in the church. Apparently all women are guilty of Eve's sin by virtue of their sex and can only be saved by childbearing. Many churches today prohibit women from being ordained or having any leadership roles in church that involve teaching men or having authority over men.

When the Timothy passage above is seen as part of a human document, it tells us how an early Christian author—a man—saw things.[8] There is much scholarship that suggests Paul, the author of Romans and Galatians, did not write this; rather, it was written by someone using Paul's name. It seems inconsistent with Paul's earlier writing in Galatians 3:28 that says, "There is no longer Jew or Greek, there is no longer slave or free, there is no longer male and female; for all of you are one in Christ Jesus." The real question is whether this passage has authority for the church today. Is this God's command or the product of cultural accommodation taking place in one early church under a specific set of circumstances?

If authority is given to Jesus' teachings such as "love your neighbor (male or female) as yourself" and "do unto others as you would have them do to you," then we are faced with a decision as to who is really the authority for what it means to be a Christian today. Is it Jesus or not? If it is Jesus, then the Timothy passage must be put aside as an example of a situation in the past where Jesus' teachings were not followed, and thus this passage is not authoritative for us today.

Weaknesses of the Hypothesis

Understanding the Bible as a collection of documents prepared by humans requires readers to devote time and attention to the context of the writing, to grant scriptural authority, to confront their past securities, and to temper the limits of interpretive license.

Context

To interpret passages for the twenty-first century, readers must take advantage of biblical scholarship and "dig deeper" to understand the passages in their historical contexts. While this is a strength of the method for those willing to expend the necessary energy, it can be discouraging for those who are accustomed to accepting the literal or conventional interpretation. The current "creationism" controversy is a good example.

The person who sees the Bible as a human document should first ask whether the Genesis creation stories were written to offer a "scientific" account of creation, or whether the writer had another purpose in mind and, if so, what would that purpose have been in the historical context in which the stories were written. This requires much more effort than simply accepting a creation story as a true scientific fact because it is in the Bible.

Authority

When understood as a collection of documents penned by human hands, scripture only has the authority granted by the reader or hearer. This model is in direct opposition to the divine oracle approach in which authority is external, or independent of the reader, and to which the reader is subject. Proponents of the divine oracle approach decry this as a major problem. They argue that if you doubt the accuracy of any part of scripture, you "don't believe the Bible"; that this is a "slippery slope" in which a failure to acknowledge the inerrancy and infallibility of any part of scripture ultimately leads to the loss of credibility of all scripture. This argument is simply not universally true. However, for some people, the requirement for personal responsibility diminishes the feeling of security that inerrancy and infallibility provide.

How we behave is the evidence or proof of the actual authority we have granted, independent of what we say we believe. For example, if I claim to be a Christian and hate my neighbor, I have acknowledged that Jesus' teachings are not the real, actual authority or standard for my behavior.

Securities
When we read that God sent a death angel to murder Egyptian children, we don't just accept that as truth, and thus give up the sense of security that everything in the Bible is truly God's inerrant word. We ask whether that story is consistent with the nature of God as taught by Jesus.

- Do God's moral values change with time?
- Did things happen just the way they are described in the Bible, or were some stories told in such a way as to attract the attention of the listener in an oral culture?
- Were these descriptions used to describe the nature of God that was common at that time?
- Are they binding on us today if they are in conflict with the teachings of Jesus?

All these questions become important when the Bible is seen as a human product. Such questions are not considered appropriate and are not discussed by people who use the divine oracle hypothesis.

Interpretation
There is a danger that the metaphorical approach will allow too much imagination, resulting in interpretations that have little to do with the historical meaning. Therefore, it must be "controlled" by the historical approach. Metaphor and history must work together.[9]

A "Sacrament of the Sacred"

The Bible gives meaning to our lives by serving as what Marcus Borg calls a "Sacrament of the Sacred." Borg describes a sacrament as a means by which we experience the presence of God or sense the presence of the

Holy Spirit. Words written long ago speak to us in meaningful ways in our present time. Even though the words were composed by imperfect human minds, just as the bread and wine in the Eucharist were made by human hands, these can mediate God's grace and love to us.[10]

Notes

[1] Marcus Borg, *Reading the Bible Again for the First Time* (New York: Harper Collins, 2001), 35.

[2] Phyllis A. Bird, "The Authority of the Bible," *The New Interpreter's Bible,* ed. L.E. Keck (Nashville: Abingdon, 1994) I: 35-36.

[3] Walter Brueggemann, *The Creative Word: Canon as a Model for Biblical Education* (Philadelphia: Fortress Press, 1982), 14.

[4] Borg, *Reading the Bible Again*, 40.

[5] Ibid., 41.

[6] Harry Emerson Fosdick, *A Guide to Understanding the Bible* (New York: Harper, 1938), 54.

[7] Borg, *Reading the Bible Again*, 39.

[8] Ibid., 25-26.

[9] Ibid., 44.

[10] Ibid., 31-33.

CRITICAL QUESTIONS AND DECISIONS

Referring to the diagram in the introduction, we have now come to decision point D1. Which of the two hypotheses about the Bible gives us the best opportunity to answer the three critical questions about the character of God, how God interacts with humanity, and what God expects of me?

Once that decision is made, the next decision point (D2) deals with what will serve as our source of authority for faith and practice. Will it be manmade creeds and doctrines or the teachings of Jesus?

After we make that decision, we will be in a position to address the three critical questions and examine how the answers affect how we understand the Christian life.

DECISION 1:
THE BIBLE IS A HUMAN PRODUCT.

Based on internal evidence, the divine oracle view of scripture cannot be credible. The Bible contains many passages that conflict with one another and that give conflicting answers to our critical questions about God and what God expects of us. The alternative is to accept the hypothesis that the Bible is a human product. Accepting this hypothesis does not deny the influence of God on the lives of the writers but says only that the authors were not coerced by God regarding what they wrote and were free to tell their stories as they thought appropriate. Accepting the Bible as a human product does not solve the problem of internal contradictions but requires that we make additional decisions relative to which passages will and will not be considered authoritative.

DECISION 2:
JESUS IS OUR AUTHORITY.

The decision to claim Jesus as our authority seems the obvious choice if one is trying to be a follower of Jesus, a Christian. Jesus' resurrection expresses God's approval of Jesus' ministry. Jesus presents to us as much of God and God's truth as can be expressed in a human being. The decision to make Jesus our authority means we make Jesus' actual teachings our authority, not some collection of propositions *about* Jesus. Having made this decision, we are now able to answer the three critical questions about the nature of God, how God deals with humanity, and what is expected of us in order to have an appropriate relationship with God. Jesus' teachings are definitive.

If we find other teachings elsewhere in scripture that are not consistent with Jesus' teachings, then these are not authoritative for us. Inherent in the idea that Jesus is our authority is that Jesus did not omit anything that was important or necessary to answer our three critical questions.

CRITICAL QUESTION 1: WHAT IS THE NATURE OF GOD?

The primary source of authority for understanding the character or nature of God is found in the life and teachings of Jesus, as recorded in all four Gospels. Jesus' characterization of God is also supported by writings found outside the Gospels. When we talk about the nature or character of God, we are not claiming to know all there is about God. We are concerned with God's attitude toward humanity and any constraints or rules that God uses when dealing with humanity, as taught by Jesus.

There are three sources for discerning the nature of God: records in the Hebrew Bible, the verbal teachings of Jesus, and the actions of Jesus. The Hebrew Bible contains many insights into the nature of God that are consistent with Jesus' teachings. The way Jesus taught and interacted with others demonstrated how he felt he could help bring about God's rule and kingdom. Both his teachings and actions illustrate what he believed was important to God, and thus reflect the nature and character of God.

Roots in the Hebrew Bible

Jesus' characterization of God as compassionate has its roots in Jewish history. The law required a remission of debts every seventh year (Deut. 15:1). This command, understood to be directly from God, along with the Jubilee (fiftieth) year stipulation that all property was to be returned to the original owner's family and indentured servants freed, helped to ensure that there would not be a permanently impoverished class in the society. Even the land was given a rest (Leviticus 25). Compassion for the poor who had little or no land was demonstrated in this part of the law:

> When you reap the harvest of your land, you shall not reap to the very edges of your field, or gather the gleanings of your harvest; you shall leave them for the poor and for the alien: I am the Lord your God. (Lev. 23:22)

The Prophets also speak about what God desires, which reflects their understanding of the compassionate nature of God:

- "For I (God) desire steadfast love and not sacrifice, the knowledge of God rather than burnt offerings" (Hos. 6:6).
- "What to me is the multitude of your sacrifices? says the Lord; I have had enough of burnt offerings of rams and the fat of fed beasts; I do not delight in the blood of bulls, or of lambs, or of goats.... learn to do good; seek justice, rescue the oppressed, defend the orphan, plead for the widow" (Isa. 1:11, 17).
- "God says, 'But let justice roll down like waters, and righteousness like an ever-flowing stream'" (Amos 5:24).

When Jesus gave the Great Commandment to love God and love your neighbor as yourself (Mark 12:29-31), both parts came from the Hebrew Bible (Deut. 6:4-6, Lev. 19:18). Jesus gleaned the best view of God from the Hebrew Bible and modified it to yield a unique and different view of God, with important consequences.

Jesus' unique view of God

While compassion for the poor and disadvantaged was an important characteristic of God in the Hebrew Bible, Jesus' picture of God does not include the doctrine of rewards and punishments, which is an integral part of the covenant relationship between the Jewish people and God, as understood by the prophets and most of the Old Testament writers (the Book of Job is an exception). Jesus specifically taught that God's love is non-preferential, "[God] makes his sun rise on the evil and on the good, and sends rain on the righteous and on the unrighteous" (Matt. 5:45).

Perhaps Jesus' most direct characterization of God is found in the parable of the loving father. In it the father, illustrating God, welcomes the wayward son, "But while he was still far off, his father saw him and was filled with compassion; he ran and put his arms around him and kissed him" (Luke 15:20). This story shows the father acting, not with offers of rewards or threats of punishment to coerce the son's behavior, but with love, mercy, and compassion. This represents a new relationship model that replaced the old covenant model and its promises of rewards and punishments (Deuteronomy 28). This will be discussed in more detail in the section on how God interacts with humanity.

Jesus' verbal teachings

Jesus' teachings about what God desires reflect the nature of God. God's desire that we love others, especially our enemies, follows directly from God's nature and character of showing mercy and working for peace.

- "Be merciful, just as your Father is merciful" (Luke 6:36).
- "You have heard that it was said, 'You shall love your neighbor and hate your enemy.' But I say to you, "Love your enemies and pray for those who persecute you, so that you may be children of your Father in heaven…" (Matt. 5:43-45).
- "Be perfect, therefore, as your heavenly Father is perfect" (Matt. 5:48).
- "Blessed are the peacemakers, for they will be called children of God" (Matt. 5:9).

Jesus' actions

How Jesus interacted with others also illustrates how he understood the nature of God. Because his mission was to show how to live out God's will, he demonstrated the types of actions that were righteous in God's sight and thus revealed the character and nature of God. The following examples illustrate the compassion of Jesus and his desire to free people from bondage of all types, both spiritual and physical:

- He healed lepers (Mark 1:40-45, Luke 17:11-19). People with leprosy were considered unclean and so were rejected by their families and community. Eliminating this disease freed them to return to their homes and families and live normal lives. In the Mark passage Jesus reaches out and touches the leper. This would have been perceived as a compassionate affirmation of the humanity of the leper.

- He healed blind people (Mark 8:8:22-26, 10:46-52; Matt. 9:27-31; John 9:1-41). Blind people were usually beggars since they could not work. Restoring their sight freed them to have the chance for a full life.

- He healed a paralyzed man (Mark 2:1-12). Jesus' first words to the man were "Your sins are forgiven." This seems a strange thing to say to a paralyzed man. However, it is likely this man thought his paralysis was a punishment from God. Jesus separated the man's physical condition from his spiritual condition. After Jesus healed the paralytic, the man left free of the burden of thinking God was punishing him and of the burden of not being able to walk and participate in the life of his family and community.

- He saved the life of a woman caught in adultery (John 8:1-11). According to Hebrew law (Lev. 20:10), this woman deserved to be put to death. Jesus had compassion, however, perhaps knowing that women were often abused and powerless in that society. His actions demonstrated his belief that loving your neighbor as yourself was God's desire and that loving someone regardless of their moral condition was part of what it meant to be a member of God's kingdom.

- He saved a Roman centurion's servant (Matt. 8:5-13). The centurion would have been considered by most people in Hebrew society as the hated enemy. Jesus was not blinded by hatred and was willing to go to the servant and help him. The centurion trusted Jesus because Jesus was known for his compassion and his desire to do God's will.

- He healed a Syrophoenician woman's daughter (Mark 7:24-30). Jesus ignored the normal code of conduct that would have forbidden him to talk to any woman in a public place, much less a gentile woman.

- He conversed with tax collectors and people considered to be sinners by the religious establishment (Mark 2:15-16, Luke 19:1-10). In the Luke passage, Zacchaeus is described as the chief tax collector. Zacchaeus had a conversion experience and Jesus said "Today salvation has come to this house, because he too is a son of Abraham." The term "son of Abraham" likely refers to Jews in general but could also refer to anyone who, like Abraham, demonstrated a commitment to follow as God commanded.

There are many other examples of healings and exorcisms that could be given. Even from these listed above, we may draw several conclusions:

- Jesus' compassion, and by extension God's compassion, is available to both men and women and to Jews and non-Jews.
- Jesus' desire to free people from whatever bondage prevented them from being able to live as full human beings is indicative of God's desire for us and thus reflects the character of God.
- Suffering in this life is not the will of God and is not due to God's actions.
- God's character never changes with time. Jesus taught nothing to the contrary.
- God's character and desire for us is perfect, selfless love.

Some followers of Jesus understood what he was trying to teach. Two of the best examples are found in John 3:16, "For God so loved the world. . ." and in 1 John 4:7-8, "Beloved, let us love one another, because love is from God; everyone who loves is born of God and knows God. Whoever does not love does not know God, for God is love."

God's will, as Jesus expressed it, follows directly from his understanding of the nature and character of God. This understanding has major implications for how Jesus perceived God interacting with humanity and on the amount of influence God can exert on humans to encourage them to do God's will.

CRITICAL QUESTION 2:
HOW DOES GOD INTERACT WITH HUMANITY?

Jesus taught that God interacts with humanity based on two principles. First, God does not interact with us coercively and therefore will not overpower our free choices in making decisions, either for good or bad. This is a consequence of God's will, to love God and neighbor. To truly love God and others, we must have free choice. Thus, God would not interact with us in a way that prevents us from having the freedom to choose. This means that God can interact with humanity to encourage us to do God's will, but the interaction will not be coercive. No coercion translates into no use of rewards and punishments. This principle implies that God's actions are self-constrained so as to preserve our ability to freely choose any course of action. In other words, God interacts with us in a way that allows us freely to choose to do God's will. This freedom has huge consequences for how we imagine God is involved in our everyday lives and whether God is somehow in control of people and events.

The second principle is one Jesus taught directly: God does not give preferential treatment (see Matt. 5:43-45). An example is found in Jesus' parable of the laborers in the vineyard (Matt. 20:1-16) where the owner pays all the laborers the same wage regardless of how long they worked. This second principle is closely related to the first since preferential treatment is inherently coercive. For example, if God healed everyone who contracted cancer but attended the Catholic church twice a week, who among us would not attend the same church twice a week and also bring our family and friends? But would we be attending church to worship God or just to receive the protection from cancer? The preferential treatment would effectively rob us of the ability to choose freely to worship.

This second principle also means that God does not interact with us through rewards and punishments. Jesus does not talk about God manipulating people and events or using physical and material rewards and punishments to coerce behavior. Thus, Jesus' vision of how God interacts with us was radically different from the covenant view described in the Hebrew Bible. Jesus gave us a new relationship model.

The old relationship model
The covenant with its laws and regulations and associated physical and material rewards and punishments dominated the relationship between God and the Hebrews. This model is very similar to that found in some ancient treaties between a powerful person such as the head of a dominant empire and a weaker nation. The powerful party laid down the conditions of the covenant and the related rewards for fidelity and punishments for infidelity.[1] It was probably the way a powerful tribal leader dealt with his people. According to this model, God gave preferential treatment in the form of physical and material rewards and punishments to coerce the Hebrew people into obedience. (For a good summary of the types of

rewards and punishments, see Deuteronomy 28. 14 verses deal with blessings and 54 deal with curses or punishments.)

The general idea of God using coercion to guide behavior is an easy extension of the way most parents try to develop good behavior in their children: by acting out of love and a desire that the children grow up to be moral and responsible people in society. Jesus rejected the parent-small child model, teaching that it is inappropriate for our relationship with God as adults.

A new relationship model

Jesus rejected the parent-small child model in favor of a parent-adult child model in which God's love is the same for everyone, without preferential treatment or coercion. A person's relationship with God is one of mutual love and respect and is based on free choice. Jesus expressed the importance of free choice in several ways:

- The people of Israel suffered the results of refusing the help God offered: "Jerusalem, Jerusalem, the city that kills the prophets and stones those who are sent to it! How often have I desired to gather your children together as a hen gathers her brood under her wings, and you were not willing!" (Matt. 23:37-38). Growing up in a rural area, Jesus knew that a mother hen cares for her brood and desires their well-being. She simply calls and they come—if and only if they are willing—it is their choice. Those who are unwilling can suffer tragic consequences.

- The story of the final judgment describes the outcome based on choosing to love others without thought of recognition or reward. Jesus went into detail with his disciples on the hardships they were likely to face if they followed him. He wanted them to know the cost so they could freely choose whether or not to follow him (Matt. 25:31-46).

- The father in the parable of the loving father neither sends his servants to drag his son home against his will nor offers his son material rewards for returning. The father does not use rewards or punishments to coerce his son's behavior. Rather, he continues to love the young man and waits for him to come home on his own free will (Luke 15:11-32).

Interestingly, the author of the Garden of Eden story (Genesis 2–3) recognized the importance of free choice. The serpent is described as the "most cunning creature which God had made." Temptation was an integral part of creation. Free choice was an essential element in the story if the adults were to be morally responsible people.

The idea that God does not interact with us based on rewards and punishments is not altogether missing in the Hebrew Bible; it is just not the dominant view. In the Book of Job, the main character argues this idea all along, else he would not be suffering. Job's friends argue that the fact Job is suffering means he is being punished by God. Near the end of the book God admonishes Job's friends, saying that Job has spoken the truth while they have not. In the Book of Jonah, God sends Jonah to Jonah's worst enemies to bring a message of God's love for them.

This idea of no rewards and punishments from God does not mean there will not be natural consequences associated with our choices. Clearly, an honest workman might receive more opportunities than a dishonest one. This does not imply that God manipulated people to bring about those opportunities. There are often internal, spiritual rewards associated with doing acts of kindness and compassion. These types of rewards are non-preferential since they are available to anyone willing to do acts of compassion. We may ask if the hypothesis that God interacts with humanity in non-preferential and non-coercive ways is supported by empirical evidence. Consider the following:

- Are Christians less likely to contract serious diseases or to be involved in traffic accidents?
- Are the innocent children of Christians immune to suffering and/or do they suffer fewer illnesses or deaths than the children of non-Christians?
- Are the prayers of Christians more effective in relieving suffering or bringing good fortune than those of non-Christians?
- Are we rewarded with good health or wealth or better parking places because we go to church and worship God?
- Are those who commit hate crimes in the name of God punished by God?
- Are wealthy people always the ones with high moral standards?
- Are the people who take advantage of others always punished?

My experience says the answer to each of these questions is an emphatic no! When I look at the lives of pastors and their families I have known who were genuinely and sacrificially devoted to God, they would be the people most likely to deserve good treatment and at least some physical and material rewards. However, I don't see any evidence of such preferential treatment or rewards. They are subject to the same misfortunes that afflict us all. All the empirical evidence confirms to me that God interacts with us in ways that are always non-preferential and non-coercive.

Jesus taught a new covenant

It is not difficult to imagine that Jesus viewed his teachings as constituting a new and different covenant when compared to that of the Hebrew Bible. The old covenant established a relationship between God and the Hebrew people based on rewards and punishments. Jesus taught a new covenant relationship with a new understanding of God as characterized by perfect love, compassion, and mercy. God desires that we freely choose to love as God loves, value others as God does, and accept that doing so will not necessarily result in any physical and material rewards in this life. God's interaction with humanity is constrained in two ways:

- God will not manipulate people in a coercive way that interferes with their freedom of choice.
- God is compassionate and merciful to all and gives no preferential treatment.

Why would I want to be a part of such a relationship? I believe that being loved and respected, not coerced and manipulated, by God gives my life value. This is the kind of relationship I have enjoyed in marriage and that has enriched my life enormously. Loving and caring for others gives my life meaning. We are designed so that we feel a sense of worth and value when we participate with God in making the world a better place for everyone in protecting our environment and in helping all creatures, human or not, that have been abused or cannot help themselves. This is what it means to be fully human as God intended.

Critical Questions and Decisions

Obviously, this new covenant is fundamentally different from that in the Hebrew Bible. Jesus brought us a radically new way of understanding and interacting with God. The divine oracle view of scripture can never acknowledge this fact.

Below are some of the consequences of this radically new way of understanding how God interacts with humanity based on non-preferential and non-coercive treatment.

- God's perfect compassion and mercy mean that God is always at work encouraging us to do God's will, but that God never violates our free will to choose to do so or not. We might think of God's encouragement coming to us much as a radio station broadcast. We are free to choose to listen and use it to strengthen our lives or to ignore it.

- God extends perfect compassion equally to every person. All people are valuable in God's sight.

- God holds nothing back. We cannot persuade God to be more compassionate or kind or merciful than God is already. This is particularly hard to accept for those of us who have been taught that prayer influences God so that God will be more benevolent than if we did not pray.

- God is not in control of people and events in our everyday lives, if by control we mean that God manipulates people and events in a coercive way.

- We must reject the use of any coercion involving the use of guilt, shame, or fear when trying to bring others, especially children, into a relationship with God.

The new covenant represents a very different way of seeing God and how God interacts with us. It may seem a little frightening at first in that it says God is not in control of everyday events. This idea of God being in control permeates much of Christianity today. One of the fundamental underlying premises of the Hebrew Bible is that God was in control of the destiny of the nation. When things were going well, God was thought to be rewarding his chosen people; when things were not going well, God must be punishing the people for their disobedience.

God was always in control. This idea was perhaps the most significant factor in the interpretation of history in the Hebrew Bible. As this history was transferred from oral form to written form, the idea of God being in control would shape the ways the writers understood God's involvement in the destiny of the nation. We can now see why the Babylonian exile was interpreted as God's punishment and King Cyrus of Persia as God's instrument to let the Hebrews return to their homeland.

Sermons rarely point out that Jesus taught a very different view of God. As the Hebrew Bible stories are told without being contrasted with Jesus' teachings, the idea of God being in control was transferred into our present-day understanding of God. This produces confusion about how God is involved in our lives.

Given God's self-imposed constraints regarding how God can deal with humanity, we can now understand why God didn't intervene and stop the Holocaust. It would have required coercion to change the minds of Hitler and his gangsters. Consider:

- If God did intervene and stop murder, shouldn't a God who values all of humanity also protect potential victims of drug overdose, distracted drivers, and so on?
- If God did stop all acts of violence or potential violence or suffering, what type of relationship could we have with such a God?
- What would happen to the freedom to choose our actions, which is the basic requirement to be able to love God and be morally responsible beings?

All the empirical data seems to confirm that God's actions are self-constrained, and this limits how God interacts with humanity.

Prayer under the new covenant
Because of the self-constraints that limit what God can do, Christianity becomes a cooperative venture with God to bring about God's kingdom.

Consider these quotes from Archbishop Desmond Tutu: "Without God, we cannot. Without us, God will not" (attributed to Saint Augustine) and "Without us, God has no eyes; without us, God has no ears; without us, God has no arms or hands. God relies on us. Won't you join other people of faith in becoming God's partners in the world?" (*God is Not a Christian*, HarperOne 2011).

According to the New Testament, Jesus often went aside to pray (Luke 3:21; 6:12; 9:18, 28; 11:1). When asked by his disciples to teach them how to pray, Jesus gave them what we call the Lord's Prayer. Our ancient Bibles do not all agree on the exact wording of the prayer, but there are a few elements that all share: praise, affirmation of the kingdom's importance and, by implication, the pray-er's participation in bringing about the Kingdom of God. There are also some requests.

The first request is for bread or daily bread. Taken literally, this could mean simply bread to eat each day. Taken metaphorically, which seems more likely, bread here means that which sustains our spiritual life—or spiritual strength that comes from a relationship with God. There is also a request for forgiveness, conditional on our own willingness to forgive others. The meaning of the last request, that God not bring the pray-er into temptation or trial, is curious since Jesus taught clearly about the compassion of God. A compassionate God would not bring anyone into temptation. Perhaps the temptation is believing that being a part of God's kingdom gives us a feeling of superiority and the power to pronounce God's judgement on others. There is no problem in expecting God to respond to these requests in a compassionate and non-preferential way. Note that there is no request for protection against physical danger or injury and no request for miraculous healing should injury occur.

Prayer for healing or freedom from addiction or prevention from bad judgement is not covered in the Lord's Prayer. All these involve God's intervention and are the ones that give us the most difficulty. Jesus taught that God's love is unconditional and that God interacts with us in ways that are non-preferential and non-coercive. Obviously this has important consequences for how we pray and what we can expect as a result of prayer. Following is a list of some of these consequences:

- God's unconditional love and grace mean that God's love and concern for us do not depend on our behavior, past or present. We never have to worry about being righteous in God's sight in order for God to be interested in our prayers.

- Neither the number nor intensity of our prayers is relevant to God's love for us or others. God's love is unconditional. God will not love us less even if we do not pray.

- We need not pray expecting that we can somehow get or focus God's attention. God is not asleep. God's unconditional love is always at work in each person's life.

- God is perfect in love and compassion. We should never think that we could somehow, through prayer, persuade God to be more benevolent than God would otherwise be.

- We need not pray expecting God to protect us, or our loved ones, from the consequences of bad choices we or others make.

- We need not pray for the "lost" person or someone exhibiting harmful behavior, expecting that God will overpower that person's will and make their behavior change.

- We need not pray expecting deliverance from the forces of nature such as flood, hurricane, illness, and disease. Nature's forces and processes are part of creation, are morally neutral, and are not manipulated by God to favor some people at the expense of others.

- We need not expect God to answer prayers that request preferential treatment. Because God loves all, God will not favor one person over another. If God arbitrarily healed one person and not another, this would be a clear indication that the one healed was of more value or importance than the one not healed. Jesus taught that God is non-preferential, not capricious.

This list might leave us with the question, why pray? Rather, it suggests that we may need to alter our expectations of what God will do as a result of our requests. This may seem hard to accept, but it is probably because we have grown up in a culture that instilled in us the idea that prayer can cause God to be more benevolent or generous or concerned than if we did not pray. Most of us have grown up in churches or have seen televised revivals where people gave testimonies about how prayer caused God to heal them of some terrible disease. Many of us have known of people who did not recover, but those cases are rarely, if ever, mentioned. We teach by omission also and, in doing so, instill unrealistic expectations and set people up for disappointment and disillusionment. How would it feel to know your loved one died of cancer while listening to a testimony about how someone else's loved one survived because of the many prayers that were offered on their behalf? The list above does not suggest that we should not pray, but it does suggest that we need to adjust how we pray and what we expect to happen as a result.

Belief in a God of compassion means that God is also saddened by suffering. God has always been active in a non-coercive way in our lives to prevent suffering. Maybe it came in a still small voice that suggested I need to get an annual checkup, have the colonoscopy I have been putting off for so many years, quit smoking, reduce my alcohol consumption, stop drinking and driving, use good judgement, cease texting while driving, etc. We need not think that because God does not act in a crisis situation that God is or has been indifferent. Perhaps we have been too busy to notice all the ways God has tried to influence our decisions.

Belief in a God of compassion also means that God desires to help the person who needs to pray. God is the parent to whom we can turn in time of trouble, the parent who will always be there, the one on whom we lean when we need love and support. By analogy, imagine I am in the waiting room alone while my loved one is at the brink of death. A dear friend comes in to be with me. I share my frustrations and fears, feelings that somehow I should have done things differently or that I should have been a better spouse—or a thousand other feelings. When I have exhausted my emotions, I will have benefited greatly, but I will not feel that I have transferred to my friend the responsibility to make sure my loved one is restored to health.

William Barclay says in his spiritual autobiography that "prayer must never be regarded as a labor-saving device." It is not a way to elude things we want to avoid, but rather a channel to find the strength to go through the hard times and be the victor instead of the victim, looking to Jesus as our example: "Jesus did not evade the Cross; he went through the Cross to the resurrection."[2]

An elderly woman in my church shared an example of this way of thinking from the time when her son was serving overseas combat duty during World War II. She said that initially she prayed every night that he would return home safely, but one night she had a revelation: "If we are to win this terrible war, a lot of our precious boys are going to die. That is just the way it has to be. If I ask God to protect my son and bring him home safely, am I not asking God to withhold protection for another mother's son?" After that revelation, she said she never prayed that way again. Not only was this a great insight, but it was also a beautiful example of what it means to love your neighbor as yourself.

Understanding how God interacts with us can be a truly freeing experience. I thought about that often as I sat with my dad through his struggle with cancer. Of course I prayed for his recovery. That was my heart's desire, and I believe in a God who listens to heartfelt prayer and shares our pain. Even though I shared with God all the reasons why my dad's life was so important, I had decided not to *expect* God to give him preferential treatment. That's right: I asked God to do what was on my heart, but didn't expect God to do it. I said many of the same things to my wife, who listened and consoled me as best she could, but I didn't expect her to take responsibility for Dad's healing. I knew what I wanted in my heart, but in my head I had concluded that it was unreasonable to ask God to do something Jesus taught us was not consistent with God's nature.

This change in my expectations has been a wonderful gift, a freeing experience. I never have to wonder if only I had a closer relationship with God or was more spiritual, somehow I could be more persuasive when asking God to be more benevolent than God would otherwise be. I never have to imagine that I need to change God's attitude. I trust that God would be doing everything possible for me or my loved one that could be done without violating the principle of non-preferential treatment.

When my dad died I never imagined his failure to recover as being punishment from God. Likewise, had he recovered, I would not have interpreted that as a reward for him or me. I never felt that God was indifferent. God refused to grant my request for preferential treatment because to do so would say, in effect, that God cared more for my dad than for others who were also dying, many of whom had people praying for them too. I know that God's spirit is always present helping all of us make the best of the situation. This is not indifference on God's part.

While prayer does not change God, it may well have a direct effect on the ones for whom we pray, especially if they know of our concern for their well-being. Knowing that we are loved certainly can have a beneficial effect. It gives us a sense of worth and value. It encourages us to return to our friends and loves ones. It gives us a reason to fight for wholeness, both mental and physical.

Glenn Hinson, a church history professor and leader in the spirituality movement, has often talked about "love energy" that can have a positive influence on the person to whom it is directed. Some research studies have claimed that people who know they are being prayed for recover more quickly than those who do not receive prayer. I believe that is possibly true, not because God does more for those who receive the prayers, but because these prayers give the object of the prayer more desire and inner strength to recover.

Before leaving this subject, we should look at Jesus' prayer in the garden just prior to his arrest (Matt. 26:36-46). There were no eyewitnesses to these events, so his followers reconstructed them. They do, however, represent the type of person they felt Jesus to be and what they believed he would have said.

Jesus prayed for God to help him avoid the cross, but if not, for God's will to be done. Many have interpreted this to mean that Jesus thought God's will was for him to go to the cross, but others believe that Jesus was expressing to God what was on his heart—fear and dread. If the cross could not be avoided, he asked that God's will be done. Jesus taught that God's will was to love God and neighbor. What was the loving thing to do?

Jesus could have escaped, but how would he have any credibility with his disciples whom he had asked to stay true to the mission, regardless of the cost? Love for others required that he not run away. Did Jesus ask for preferential treatment? Yes. Did he expect that God would comply? No. He knew his mission was to do God's will and help bring about the Kingdom of God, regardless of the personal cost.

So why pray? There are two main reasons. First we pray to share our heart's desires, fears, and joys with God because God cares about our well-being. That is a part of the meaning of a relationship with God. Second, we pray because we are the ones who need to change. God does not need to change. We use prayer to hear God's voice, to align our thinking with Jesus' teachings about God's will and about how we can act to help make the world the type of place that would be pleasing to God. This includes how we should act with all those with whom we come into contact. We pray because we need to be intentional about being loving people, especially with those who are not loving toward us or our loved ones and those who don't share our values. Prayer is a primary means of our transformation.

One thing not to worry about
Again using Jesus as our authority and guide, there is one issue that was very important in the past that we no longer have to worry about: the confusing issue about the internal nature of God, or the Trinity. This is often a prominent component in propositional statements that people are called on to profess. The writer of John's gospel has Jesus say that "I and the Father are one" (John 10:30). The early church seems to have taken this literally and thus began an acrimonious debate on the relationship between God and Jesus, and that later included the Holy Spirit. People were put to death because of disagreement over what this and similar statements actually meant. Jesus never said anything like that in the other three gospels. He was certainly one with the Father in terms of purpose and goal of his mission. Regardless, Jesus never required that his followers believe he was both human and divine.

In his book, *The Heart of Christianity*, Marcus Borg has an excellent discussion about the pre-Easter Jesus, the flesh-and-blood person who lived and died, and the post-Easter Jesus, the Jesus of faith in the early church and how the Gospels record a mixture of both. This is helpful in understanding how the portrayal of Jesus can be so different in the various gospels and in seeing why failure to distinguish between the two can degrade our understanding of both.[3]

For new covenant believers, Jesus is our authority by virtue of the resurrection that was God's seal of approval. If believing that Jesus was divine helps us to do God's will, that is a good thing. But we cannot denigrate those who do not need Jesus' divinity as a necessary component of their devotion to doing the will of God.

CRITICAL QUESTION 3: WHAT DOES GOD EXPECT OF ME?

Jesus clearly taught, in what he called the "greatest and first commandment" and "a second like it," that doing God's will is expected of anyone who desires to have an appropriate relationship with God.

God's will is the same for everyone, perhaps again an aspect of non-preferential love. What determines our interests and skills is partly genetic and partly nurture, culture, and environment. They are not direct, personal, preferential gifts from God. We often hear language to the effect that specific talents are gifts from God. In an indirect way, considering God as creator and sustainer of our universe, all things are gifts from God, but using this language often causes confusion because it implies that God gives special treatment to some and not to others.

The citizens of a kingdom are those who live under the reign of the king. Those who live under God's reign are members of God's kingdom, and thus live according to God's will. Jesus invited all of us to be citizens in the Kingdom of God.

I remember being told as a young person that God had a plan for my life. When I asked what that was, I was told it was up to me to find out. Since I had no clue, I found this idea very frustrating. Why couldn't God just tell me? Was I going to be miserable until I discovered the right path? It was like being told I had a map to a great treasure, only to see that the path was marked in invisible ink. This did not help my relationship with God. Many years later I discovered that Jesus had already given me God's will for my life. It was the Great Commandment: to love God and my neighbor as myself. Even if I couldn't feel love, the Golden Rule—

"Do to others as you would have them do to you" (Matt. 7:12, Luke 6:31)—told me how to act. This rule does not say "Don't do to others if you don't want it done to you." The love Jesus taught is not passive but active, not negative but affirmative.

How do we love a God we cannot see or touch? Jesus' formulation of the Great Commandment provides the answer. Jesus said that the first commandment is to love God, but the second, to love your neighbor, is "like unto it." How are they alike? Because they both involve love. That is true, but they are alike in a deeper way. Jesus taught that God is compassionate, which means that God suffers when we suffer. But God is self-limited in how much God will do. So when we reduce the suffering of our neighbors, we reduce the suffering of God. In other words, God feels the love we show to others and accepts that as an expression of our love for God.

DECISION 3:
ACCEPT JESUS' UNDERSTANDING OF SALVATION.

When I was growing up I heard a lot about sin and how we all needed to repent—that is, to stop sinning—or else we were doomed to eternal hell. The solution for this terrible condition, and to secure my place in heaven rather than hell, was to be forgiven. In fact, the main reason I wanted to become a Christian was to make sure I could go to heaven. To be forgiven, I only had to profess belief in a particular doctrine about what Jesus accomplished by dying on the cross—a doctrine theologians call Penal Substitutionary Atonement (PSA).

Around 1100 CE a man named Anselm, the Bishop of Canterbury, introduced this doctrine into the Catholic Church. He explained this way of understanding the death of Jesus in his book, *Cur Deus Homo*, and his interpretation has dominated much of Christianity since. According to this doctrine, Jesus died in my place (substitution) to appease God's demand for just punishment for sin (penal). Once payment had been made, God would be willing to forgive my sin (atonement), provided I professed belief in the doctrine. This is propositional salvation and has been a dominant theme in Christian churches for hundreds of years.

While Jesus took sin seriously, he saw the basic problem differently. The chart below, adapted from Borg, is helpful in comparing the conventional understanding of propositional salvation to that of Jesus' new covenant approach:

	Propositional Salvation	New Covenant Salvation
Goal	Get to heaven	Be born again
Problem	Sin	Bondage
Solution	Forgiveness	Freedom, liberation
Requirement	Belief in penal substitutionary atonement;l	Transformation through repentance and doing God's will

For Jesus, sin was not the fundamental problem, but a symptom of a deeper problem. This can be seen in the stories of his encounters with the Jewish leader Nicodemus and the tax collector Zacchaeus.

When Jesus met Nicodemus he said "Very truly, I tell you, no one can see the kingdom of God without being born from above" (John 3:3). Jesus said, in effect, the goal is to be born again so that you can be a citizen of God's kingdom.

The problem is not just that you sin, but that you want to sin. The fundamental problem is bondage. Bondage produces the desire to sin. This could be addiction, desire for money and power, lust, jealousy, etc. The solution to bondage is not forgiveness but freedom—freedom through repentance and trust in Jesus' teachings. Forgiveness follows the change of heart and mind, as Jesus taught in the Disciples' Prayer, or as we know it the Lord's Prayer.

When Zacchaeus declared how he would now treat others, Jesus said that "salvation has come to this house" (Luke 19:1-10). Zacchaeus had repented and his life was now guided by a new principle, the Great Commandment. He was free of his bondage to the compulsion to acquire wealth and power. Once he was free of his bondage, he lost the desire to sin. This is how he would be able to understand God's kingdom and be a part of it.

Jesus began his ministry with the proclamation that "The time is fulfilled, and the kingdom of God has come near; repent, and believe in the good news." Repentance meant turning and going in a new moral and spiritual direction. What was the good news? It clearly was not how bad a sinner we are and that God is going to send us to hell for eternity. The good news meant that God loves everyone equally and unconditionally, treats everyone the same, is compassionate, does not treat us coercively or preferentially, and desires only that we live by the Great Commandment. That is really good news. In this context, to repent meant to turn and go down a different spiritual path. First, trust in the God that Jesus taught. Second, make the Great Commandment and the Golden Rule life's guiding principles.

It is important to note that nowhere does Jesus make salvation conditional on professing assent to any propositions about himself. Even in John's gospel the "I am" sayings of Jesus are not requirements he laid down, but rather were statements that John's community believed to be true. It was the church that later made these statements into propositional requirements. Being "saved" based on assent to propositions about Jesus was an invention of the early church and today has become almost synonymous with being Christian. This propositional salvation has been ruinous for Christianity.

The murder and suffering caused by the church were orchestrated by people who professed all the "right" things about Jesus. Many people who owned slaves in this country believed they were Christians and "saved," as they professed all the right things. Propositional salvation has told people their eternal destiny is secure while leaving them in bondage. Where was the white 'Christian" community during the civil rights movement? Were they on the side of equal treatment, justice, and dignity for all? Propositional salvation does not necessarily produce a changed heart. It has become a perversion of Jesus' message and has created an orthodox, acceptable way to avoid obeying the Great Commandment.

How can I begin this process of salvation that Jesus taught? From Jesus' example we could surmise that it is a combination of his own desire and the work of the Holy Spirit. By Holy Spirit, I mean the voice of God that encourages and leads us toward doing God's will, but always without being coercive or overpowering our ability to make free choices. This process is thus a cooperative one. Robert Brizee, in his book, *Where in the World is God?* suggests a picture I have found helpful in understanding this concept.

Imagine that each moral decision I make is preceded by an internal "council meeting" at a table where the council members are made up of influences from my body's senses, memories of teachings by people important in my life, voices from my culture or surroundings, perceived immediate circumstances, religious and secular education, and the independent, unfiltered voice of God. I am seated at the table listening to all these voices and influences, and I also have a built-in, internal, receiver capable of receiving this message from God. God's voice suggests how I might actually do God's will in this situation. I might feel a sense of "ought-ness" about how I should behave in this situation. The voice of God is always there whether I hear it above the others or not.

Repentance means learning to hear that voice of God above all the others. This process happens many times a day, for big decisions and often for small ones. Prayer, or listening to God, can play a major role here. I suspect that Jesus spent considerable time listening *to* God and listening *for* God. God suggests how our actions could contribute to reducing the suffering, both physical and emotional, of those in crisis by expressing care for someone in a meaningful way, speaking an encouraging word, extending hospitality, being sensitive to treat others the way we would want to be treated. We ultimately must make the commitment to do it.

JUDGMENT AND THE "FAITH VS. WORKS" DEBATE

Virtually anyone who has grown up in church has heard the statement, "We are saved by faith and not by works." This controversy apparently arose after the definitions of "saved," "faith," and "works" had been changed from those used when Jesus taught his followers.

Works originally meant actually doing the things Jesus taught were appropriate to do God's will. Martin Luther seems to have misinterpreted "works," as used in the book of James, where it says, "faith without works is dead" (Jas. 2:26). Faith originally meant genuine trust in Jesus that results in acts of love and compassion, as Jesus taught. It is likely that for Luther, "works" meant deeds done or money given to the church to "cancel" sin and secure forgiveness—transactional salvation practiced by the Catholic Church in Luther's time. Luther was correct in saying that Jesus never considered works of this type to be appropriate. For Jesus, the motivation must be unselfish love—not a self-centered desire for eternal security.

If being "saved" means that we are genuinely engaged in the process of transformation, and "works" means being intentional about transformation and actively engaged in doing the things Jesus taught, then works can indeed produce salvation—as in the story of Zacchaeus.

Motivation behind doing acts of compassion is very important. In the parable of the last judgment (Matt. 25:31-46), Jesus says that those judged righteous are the people who visit prisoners, welcome strangers, feed the hungry, bring fresh water for the thirsty, and clothe the naked. All these "works" are performed out of love, the unselfish desire for the well-being of another person. The people who benefit from these acts of love will probably never be able to repay the acts of kindness. People who love in this unselfish way are in the process of transformation that leads to salvation. Jesus said that when acts of compassion and love are done for the less fortunate, he would consider them as acts of love and compassion done to him—without expectation of a reward in the present. People obsessed with acting toward others for personal benefit are still in bondage.

Jesus never used "faith" as belief in propositions about himself. For Jesus, "faith" meant trust. Recall his comment about the centurion: ". . . in no one in Israel have I found such faith" (Matt. 8:10-13). Believing propositions about Jesus are not necessarily bad but can never replace the necessity of doing God's will.

What type of judgment will we experience at death? Considering the teachings of Jesus about the nature of God, surely it will not be based on purely punitive justice, that is, punishment for what we have done or not done. God's compassion and love suggest that it will be restorative justice.

We are all in bondage to some extent, and our self-deception prevents us from recognizing this fact. Perhaps our judgement consists of stripping away self-deception so that we see ourselves as God sees us. We then can see plainly all we have done or not done and will judge ourselves. We sometimes experience a bit of this when we lose a loved one and judge ourselves based on what we have said and done, or what we have neglected to do. This type of judgment is often more severe than anything others would impose.

I hope that a merciful God would allow some path for restoration and forgiveness so that we can somehow feel worthy to be in the presence of God and others whose lives we have touched. I have no idea how this could work, but it is at least consistent with the nature of God that Jesus taught. I don't believe that a loving God would condemn anyone to an eternity of pain and suffering with no hope of reconciliation.

Notes

[1] John Dominic Crossan, *How to Read the Bible & Still be a Christian* (New York: Harper, 2015), 14.

[2] William Barclay, *William Barclay—A Spiritual Autobiography* (Grand Rapids: Eerdmans, 1975), 53-54.

[3] Marcus Borg, *The Heart of Christianity* (New York: Harper, 2003), 80-100.

CONCLUSION

In the beginning of this study I proposed that there are three interconnected questions we need to answer if we are to have a meaningful relationship with God:

1. What is the character of God?
2. How does God interact with humanity?
3. What does God expect of me?

As someone who grew up in church and attended almost every worship service, I am sad to say that I was a middle-aged adult before I could answer these three questions with any degree of certainty. I had done what I was told to make sure I got to heaven and avoided hell. I wore the label "Christian" but had only a hint of what that really meant.

When I now think about having a personal relationship with God, I don't see how that would be possible without having some coherent answers to these questions. My early church training did not provide those coherent answers. The decision-making process outlined above evolved over many years and now seems so logical that I don't know why it was not common knowledge.

When we look at Jesus' life and ministry, we might ask why Jesus spent his ministry teaching and demonstrating the type of love he believed that God desired to see in our lives. He could have taught international relations or how to survive in an occupied country or any number of topics that addressed the more immediate political problems of his day. Instead, Jesus spent virtually his entire ministry teaching that God wanted us to exhibit a special type of love—agape—unselfish, self-sacrificing, and compassionate. This kind of love moves people to act for the benefit of others without regard to any possible reciprocal action or physical or material benefit and is not dependent on family ties. We see this in the way Jesus interacted with others, restoring the lives of perfect strangers without regard to the possibility of reciprocal action or reward.

Why is agape love so important? One possible explanation that makes sense comes from what may seem a strange confluence of factors.

First, I am not aware of examples of this agape love exhibited in the animal world. When have you heard of a lion returning a young gazelle to its mother or a wolf leading a young buffalo or elk back to the herd when it had gotten lost? The weak, lame, and vulnerable whom God said we should take care of are the preferred victims in the animal world. A mother animal may protect her young but not the young of a mother outside her family or pack. The animal world evolved to propagate each species through self-centered or family-centered actions.

Second, I see myself as a composite creature, part animal and part spiritual. Assuming the truth of the hypothesis that human animals evolved from lower animals, I see no reason to assume that I would have inherited the capacity for agape love when it doesn't exist in the animal world. Thus, this capacity and even the desire to act toward others with agape love must have come from outside, from a source independent of the evolutionary process. Interestingly in the first creation account in Genesis, God looks at the animal world that has just been created and says, "Let us make mankind in our image." Now scholars will, no doubt, scoff at this interpretation, but it is not hard to imagine the writer of that creation story seeing humankind as composite creatures, part animal but endowed with something God-like—the capacity to love in a way beyond what would otherwise be possible.

Third, I have personally experienced such love and have seen it being shared by others in many different ways: Volunteers work at feeding centers for the homeless and help rehabilitate wounded veterans. People minister to strangers addicted to drugs or alcohol. Men and women rush into burning buildings to rescue others, with little or no regard for their own safety. I have experienced feelings of peace and "rightness" and inner joy when I have participated in agape love activities. I hear the same feelings expressed by others, some of whom don't see themselves as religious people. These feelings seem to come about simply as a result of how we are made—strange blends of animal and spiritual, whether we recognize it or not.

I believe that Jesus taught the need for agape love because without it we run the risk of descending into a true Godless form of purely animal existence. Without it we reject being made in God's image, which is ultimately a rejection of God. One only has to study history or watch the news or particular television series or movies to see examples of how people live who have rejected their connection to God and God's love and behave like animals. Jesus taught the importance of agape love because he believed that God wanted us to rise above our self-centered animal nature, to live with a higher moral standard. This is our ultimate worship: to love God and humanity, just as God has loved us.

Jesus taught that loving God and neighbor with this God-like agape love is the essential criterion for living in God's will. Being "Christian"—that is, a follower of Jesus—is not a label or title to be conferred by a religious organization based on criteria it invented. Looking back over Christian history, this practice has been disastrous in that it provided a way for people to think they were Christians and be assured of eternal reward without regard to whether they followed the actual teachings of Jesus. One of the greatest examples of this is the Spanish Inquisition.

Supported by the Catholic Church and led by local clergy, it was institutionalized terror, bigotry, intolerance, and anti-semitism. Thousands of people were burned alive—men, women, and children. Property was confiscated from those accused to help pay the inquisitors and witnesses against them. How could a supposedly Christian religion completely ignore the teachings of Jesus to love one's neighbor? What kind of "Christian education" would allow people to support torture, mutilation, and murder of their neighbors? There were also inquisitions in many European kingdoms. After the Reformation, Protestants and Catholics fought each other in bitter conflicts. In America the Puritans hanged "witches."

While the worst abuses have been eliminated, the problem remains. Where was the "Christian" church, particularly in the South, during the time of slavery or during the lynchings of the twentieth century? Has the Christian church consistently advocated for social justice and equality? Sadly, the answer is no; the Christian church has repeatedly defined Christianity in such a way that Jesus' teachings were largely irrelevant. In too many cases Christian is a title conferred on someone by a religious group. It is much like the title of general, senator, or president that people retain regardless of whether they actually carry out the responsibilities associated with that office. In the early church, the term Christian referred to a person with a commission, a calling, a life-long commitment to certain moral principles. Christian behavior has too often been based more on cultural norms and preservation of power than on what Jesus taught. This hypocrisy has turned many people away from the church. How do we reverse this situation and recover Jesus' definition of "Christian"?

We need to develop and implement a program of Christian education for all ages that embodies the following principles:

- Jesus is our authoritative source for what it means to be Christian, not doctrines or creeds made primarily of propositional statements *about* Jesus.
- The life and teachings of Jesus reveal the nature of God, how God interacts with us, and what God expects of us.
- The definition of Christian faith is trusting that what Jesus taught was true, essential, and authoritative.
- To "have faith" means to live according to the principles Jesus taught.
- God is and has always been consistent in love, compassion, mercy, and forgiveness.
- God loves every person regardless of moral condition, and treats us all as equally important.
- God is not indifferent, cruel, vengeful, or coercive, and does not give preferential treatment to anyone in this life.
- God's desire or will for each of us is that we love God and our neighbors as ourselves. We should treat others as we would like to be treated.
- God considers acts of love and compassion given to others, especially the disadvantaged, as love for God.
- Prayer doesn't change God. It helps us be sensitive to the work of the Holy Spirit.

- The Holy Spirit helps us in non-coercive ways to understand God's love and how to do God's will—namely, to love God and others.
- Salvation means being transformed in heart and mind, dedicated to doing God's will and making the world a better place for all creation.
- Always teach scripture in light of Jesus' teachings. When passages contradict Jesus' teachings, explain that these represent old views no longer acceptable to followers of Jesus.
- Never teach anything that the student must "unlearn" later.

Jesus demonstrated genuine commitment to love God and love others. To understand and incorporate the teachings of Jesus into our lives is what it means to be a follower of Jesus. After Jesus' death and resurrection his followers were known as people of the way, that is, the way of Jesus. My hope is that Christianity can reclaim Jesus' way, even though today it is the way less traveled.

As you go, may the Lord Jesus Christ go ahead of you as planner and preparer of your way . . . But most of all, as you go, may the Lord Jesus Christ be in you, incarnating his love now and forevermore.

www.ingramcontent.com/pod-product-compliance
Lightning Source LLC
Chambersburg PA
CBHW071012160426
43193CB00012B/2022